THE INTERNATIONAL JOURNAL OF ETHICAL LEADERSHIP

Volume 10
Summer 2023

The International Journal of Ethical Leadership
Case Western Reserve University
Editor-in-Chief: Shannon E. French, Inamori Professor in Ethics and
　Director, Inamori International Center for Ethics and Excellence
Executive Editor: Michael Scharf, Dean of the School of Law, John
　Deaver Drinko-Baker & Hostetler Professor of Law, and Director,
　Frederick K. Cox International Law Center
Senior Executive Editor: Beth Trecasa, Associate Director,
　Inamori International Center for Ethics and Excellence
Copyeditor: Thea Ledendecker

The International Journal of Ethical Leadership, Volume 10, Summer 2023

All new material © 2023 *The International Journal of Ethical Leadership*.

All rights reserved • Manufactured in the United States of America

ISSN 2326-7461
ISBN: 978-1-62922-272-1

For additional information, please contact inamoricenter@case.edu
or visit case.edu/inamori

Contents

Letters
Message from the Editor, Shannon E. French   1

Articles
Madeline Chung, "End-of-Life Visitation Guidelines during Pandemic Times"   3

Nikki Coleman, "Moral Courage: When the 'Line in the Sand' Demands a Response"   15

Sospeter Muchunguzi, "Leader-Follower Relational Dynamics for Sustained Ethical Leadership: A Leader-Member Exchange Perspective"   33

Fabio Q. B. da Silva, Mykyta Storozhenko, and Lucas Maciel, "Ethical (Mis)-Alignments in AI Systems and the Possibility of Mesa-Optimizations"   40

Caroline Walsh, "The Military Hierarchy Experience: Ethical Leadership Issues from the View of the Lower Ranks"   54

Symposia
Corrylee Drozda, Richard Herman, and Girma Parris, "Becoming a U.S. Citizen: Ethics and Justice in the Immigration System," November 28, 2022   67

Dorothy E. Roberts with Colette Ngana, "Killing the Black Body: The Urgency of Reproductive Justice," October 11, 2022   95

Transcripts
Talking Foreign Policy Transcripts
    February 21, 2023 broadcast:
    What Went Wrong in Afghanistan?   108

Contributors   130

Message from the Editor

Shannon E. French, Inamori Professor in Ethics
Director,
Inamori International Center for Ethics and Excellence,
Case Western Reserve University

Dr. Kazuo Inamori, the visionary leader who showed how valuing people above profit can produce both human flourishing and financial success, passed from this life in August of 2022. The Inamori Foundation, which he founded, generously endowed both the Inamori International Center for Ethics and Excellence and for this journal. While Dr. Inamori can never be replaced, he leaves behind a profound and meaningful legacy, encouraging us all to commit ourselves to ethics and altruism and always try to "Do the right thing as a human being." We will continue to honor him by pursuing our mission to explore ethical issues from a global perspective and nurture a deeper understanding of our common humanity. In our next volume, we will further reflect on Dr. Inamori's philosophies on and practices of ethical leadership.

The Inamori Center was also saddened by the unexpected passing last year of Dr. Paul Farmer, who had been selected to receive the 2022 Inamori Ethics Prize. Since the prize cannot be awarded posthumously, we chose not to present it to anyone else, but instead to honor his life's work combating injustice in healthcare with a series of events throughout the academic year—Conversations on Justice: Inequities in Healthcare. This volume includes one of these conversations, The Urgency of Reproductive Justice, featuring distinguished Prof. Dorothy E. Roberts in conversation with emerging scholar Colette Ngana.

In addition, you will find in this volume of the *International Journal for Ethical Leadership*:
- A transcript of a November 28, 2022, conversation between student leaders and community leaders about ethics and justice in the US immigration system and what is involved in becoming a citizen in the United States,
- A transcript of the February 21, 2023, episode of the NPR radio show *Talking Foreign Policy*, exploring the ethics of the invasion,

occupation, and recent withdrawal from Afghanistan: "What Went Wrong in Afghanistan?"
- An article from Brazilian scholar Dr. Fabio Silvia and his co-authors (including his son, an emerging scholar and student at Case Western Reserve University) on ethical issues in the development of Artificial Intelligence (AI),
- An article from Australian scholar Dr. Nikki Coleman on the essential virtue of moral courage,
- An article from CWRU alumna, Madeline Chung, addressing thorny issues with end-of-life visitation guidelines during the pandemic,
- An article from Tanzanian scholar, Sospeter Muchunguzi, on the dynamics necessary for sustained ethical leadership between a leader and their followers, and,
- An article from US Coast Guard veteran Caroline Walsh, exploring how hierarchy in the military affects ethical leadership, with some views from the lower ranks.

We hope you will find the range of perspectives captured in these pieces engaging and enlightening. The Inamori Center is charged with creating internationally recognized programs and initiatives devoted to ethical inquiry in both its practical and theoretical aspects and to facilitating the development of future leaders who will, in the words of Dr. Inamori, "serve humankind through ethical deeds rather than actions based on self-interest and selfish desires." With every issue of IJEL, our aim is to contribute to and stimulate diverse conversations that will help bring us closer to a more just and equitable future; a future where every person can depend on having rights, respect for their dignity, and a chance to thrive.

End-of-Life Visitation Guidelines during Pandemic Times

Madeline Chung

> *Endings matter, not just for the person but, perhaps even more, for the ones left behind.*
> —Dr. Atul Gawande, Being Mortal: Medicine and What Matters in the End

Introduction

Since the start of the pandemic, more than one million Americans have died of COVID-19, and many of these victims experienced death and dying alone, isolated from those who love them because hospitals and other institutions that specialize in hospice or palliative care would not allow family visits. As more dangerous and more contagious variants of the virus emerged over the last three years, hospitals have considered adopting even more restrictive "no-visitor" policies. Those in favor of stricter regulations seek to not only mitigate the introduction and transmission of COVID-19 within hospitals and their local communities, but also to preserve personal protective equipment (PPE) for health workers (Munshi et al., 2020). However, well-intended safety restrictions on visitation can inadvertently increase the levels of suffering, distress, grief, and tragedy that overwhelmingly devastate isolated patients, bereaving families, and distressed care providers (Downar & Kekewich, 2021). In this paper, I argue that medical institutions must be urged to adopt more accommodating end-of-life visitation policies while strictly implementing PPE safeguards and continuously monitoring COVID-19 prevalence in the community. Ultimately, I aim to demonstrate the importance of implementing more compassionate leadership surrounding visitor policies and more ethical initiatives that support person-centered emergency preparedness and crisis response plans.

Not-So-Helpful Public Health Protections

Healthcare teams have always dedicated their time and effort to tirelessly providing optimal care for patients, especially in hospice and palliative care settings where effective pain and symptom management requires high levels of attention. With the alarming severity of COVID-19 symptoms and shortage of medical resources, end-of-life care responsibilities have become more important than ever before. Now clinicians must also face the additional stress of finding an appropriate solution to the moral dilemma of limiting viral exposure while also finding a way to safely integrate familial support in clinical settings. The National Academy of Medicine asserts the importance that "family and/or [designated support persons] are not kept an arm's length away as spectators but participate as integral members of their loved one's care team" (Frampton et al., 2020). Growing scientific evidence has consistently demonstrated significant emotional and psychological benefits for patients, family members, and care providers when designated support persons are able to remain at the bedside throughout the course of treatment and/or during the transition to comfort care measures (Frampton et al., 2020). Erring on the side of caution, however, hospitals across the nation have implemented strictly enforced limitations or complete restrictions on family presence in many clinical care settings (Frampton et al., 2020).

This seemingly unprecedented precautionary measure is not new for the intersection of medicine and public health. In the past, hospitals enforced "no visitation" regulations to prevent outbreaks of respiratory viruses like the seasonal influenza (Nassar et al., 2018; Salgado et al., 2002). These rules progressively relaxed not only because policymakers discovered compelling amounts of evidence that showed the beneficial effects of having family present with patients during their hospital stays, but also because researchers found no significant difference in the number of healthcare-acquired infections (HAIs) or septic complications between hospitals with restrictive visitation policies and hospitals with more liberal ones (Goldfarb et al., 2017; Nassar et al., 2018). Additionally, before visitation restrictions and high standards of PPE guidelines were implemented in Wuhan, China, to help prevent an uncontrolled transmission of COVID-19, investigators found that healthcare-acquired infections accounted for a third of all cases, but 98% of these occurrences were caused by hospital staff, not visiting family members or friends (Downar & Kekewich, 2021; Zhou et al., 2020). Strictly enforced "no-visitor" policies are well-intentioned, but studies are not showing a significant difference between restrictive and liberal visitation policies in protecting patients, staff, and the public from viral exposure. Despite there being limited evidence to support the idea that visitors would contribute significantly to a hospital-related transmission of COVID-19, most healthcare institutions have still not made policy adjustments to increase daily, in-person visitation.

Rather than making efforts to systematize a safe reintroduction of family presence, a focus has been placed on offering families daily access to their loved ones through video meetings or phone calls, which can help reduce, but not eliminate, the risks associated with patient isolation if facilitated properly. Many physicians, nurses, and other bedside clinicians have been too overwhelmed with pandemic-influenced duties to reliably accomplish this task, resulting in a substantial number of unintended and disturbing emotional and psychological consequences for patients and families (Nassar et al., 2018). To resolve this, hospitals will not only have to hire and train new patient caregivers or repurpose staff such as certified nurse assistants to manage and ensure that regular and equitable patient-family communication is taking place for all patients, but they must also make sure to have a strong supply of e-communication devices (Leiter & Gelfand, 2021). Big tech companies like Apple, Amazon, and Google could provide technology as an incentive for hospitals to hire new staff to meet patients' communication needs, but this collaborative partnership would only be successfully facilitated by well-resourced hospitals (Kuntz at al., 2020). In order to improve equity, state and federal governments would have to provide the financial support that is needed for less privileged and poorly resourced care centers to both expand patient access to e-communication devices and increase numbers of appropriately compensated healthcare staff.

Even if these critical healthcare staffing shortages and device limitations were nonissues, replacing in-person visits with e-communication is not an appropriate substitute when dealing with extremely complex and often distressing end-of-life situations and discussions. Studies have shown that some patients and families do not feel comfortable articulating questions or expressing their thoughts and wishes in virtual conferences where privacy and confidentiality might not be guaranteed (Munshi et al., 2020; Kuntz et al., 2020). These communication-related challenges can result in physicians struggling to fully or properly assess a patient's needs and values, or families not getting the opportunity to share meaningful conversations with their loved ones. Moreover, the variability in scheduling meetings can make it difficult to hold impromptu conversations should patients take sudden and unexpected turns for the worse, stripping away the chance for people to spend those final, valuable moments of time and life together as a family (Kuntz et al., 2020).

Even when arrangements can be made for families to be present before and at the time of their loved one's death, these e-meetings are not always helpful or therapeutic. On the contrary, watching a loved one dying alone on a screen is often such an incredibly guilt-inducing and disturbingly inhumane experience that families are left to face increased risks of prolonged depression and intense, complicated grief (Mayland et al., 2020; Otani et al., 2017). To make matters worse, pandemic-related challenges with staffing shortages and increased demand for e-communication resources from other patients and families have resulted in bereaved family members having to say their virtual goodbyes with a time constraint (Najeeb, 2020). Family inclusion, sensitivity, and respect for grief or other mourning practices and rituals are vitally important to end-of-life practices and to each family member's emotional and mental health outcomes. For these reasons, it is indisputably unacceptable for healthcare facilities to continue operating with virtual meetings as replacements for in-person visitation, not to mention how poorly facilitated, unorganized, and inconsistent the scheduling process can be at times. Care teams must not allow loved ones to become afterthoughts, especially now that people are struggling with social isolation measures, a lack of usual support structures, and a shortage of mental health services.

Devastating Decisions: Dying Alone or Dying at Home?

The standard of care has to center around family visits and communication, not only because there is a duty to promote emotional and psychological well-being, but also because the harms of isolation are intensified for acute and critically ill patients with COVID-19, especially as they approach those final few days before death. When flexible visitor policies and encouraging family-centered care interventions are used in the ICU, patients experience reduced delirium, greater patient satisfaction, better mental health outcomes, and shorter in-patient stays (Munshi et al., 2020; Nassar et al., 2018; Goldfarb et al., 2017). Visitor restrictions only serve to increase the frequency and intensity of delirium and anxiety, which is common for patients with COVID-19 and contributes to extended hospital stays and higher risks of death (Munshi et al., 2020; Helms et al., 2020). Patients in facilities with strong visitor restrictions also experienced delays in receiving medications, lower chances of psychological recovery, difficulties leaving the bed on their own, treatment or discharge plans that have less alignment with and regard for their personal values and preferences, and severe traumatization upon separation for those with cognitive impairment (Munshi et al., 2020; Zeh et al., 2020). With the benefits and risks associated with family presence restrictions in mind, many individuals with serious symptoms of illness have made the decision to reject acute hospital care and stay at home where they can be with their loved ones as they go through the death and dying process.

Although the benefits of being surrounded by family members are emotionally and clinically significant, there is a predictable and consistent presentation of end-of-life symptoms that can eventually become unsustainably burdensome for the patient, family member, and community care services to manage, making the decision to stay at home rather than go to a palliative care facility particularly distressing (Downar & Kekewich, 2021). The condition of dying is characterized by the human mind and body's progressive deceleration, where people become weaker and bedbound, struggle to swallow food or fluids, sleep more, feel more confused or agitated, and finally decline in responsiveness until they enter a coma, which is a state of complete unresponsiveness (Ting et al., 2020). People who are dying of COVID-19 often have a rapid development of respiratory failure and hypoxia, resulting in a more rapid deterioration and death (Ting et al., 2020). Managing distressing symptoms can be challenging and even overwhelming without help from healthcare professionals who can administer comfort care treatments when needed, but it is too unthinkable for some patients and loved ones who do not want to be separated (Ting et al., 2020). If our healthcare systems work to preserve family engagement, then people would not be forced to choose between sharing meaningful connections with loved ones before the moment of death and having a well-monitored palliative care plan that reduces end-of-life suffering.

While the significance of family visits and communication is recognized, not all hospitals or medical centers have made the same efforts to develop new policies that demonstrate a commitment to preserving family presence and mitigating the risks of patient isolation. Lacking a universally agreed-upon pandemic preparedness plan has resulted in high levels of variability for visitor restrictions, even "from hospital to hospital [within] the same neighborhood," but "the opportunity to hold a dying family member's hand" cannot be determined by which ER an ambulance happened to take a patient to (Leiter & Gelfand, 2021). Knowing the profound effects that visitation policies have on levels of "patient advocacy, feeding, mobility, orientation, emotional support in settings of delirium, cognitive impairment, language barriers, end-of-life care, labor and delivery, and transitions to critical care," we must consider allowing family members to be with their loved ones (Munshi et al., 2020). Inconsistencies in these policies have caused acute care facilities with fewer restrictions and a stronger emphasis in delivering patient-centered care to face an increased burden of patient management due to more incoming transfers and patient/family reluctance about transitioning to facilities that provide palliative care but have greater restrictions (Leiter & Gelfand, 2021). Moving forward, we must find new ways of implementing more consistent visitation guidelines that not only reduce value conflicts between healthcare professionals and patients/families, but also demonstrate greater levels of compassion and respect for dying patients and grieving families, even and especially during pandemic times.

Reducing Moral Distress for Clinicians

Visitation restrictions are associated with significant risks not only to patients and families, but also to healthcare professionals. Studies have revealed that hospital staff either internalize or express "deep regret and symptoms of anxiety or depression about the COVID-19 visitor restrictions" (Munshi et al., 2020; Azoulay et al., 2020). Knowing that many "patients in their final days and hours are often minimally responsive and unable to interact with family members," hospitals must recognize that visitations must be permitted throughout a patient's hospital stay, not just potentially offered as an exception only at the moment of imminent death (Downar & Kekewich, 2021). Moreover, with the unpredictability of prognostication due to sudden patient deterioration and death that sometimes takes place without the expected warning signs, scheduling an end-of-life visit can be extremely challenging, and this often results in "family members were forced to leave the bedside of patients who appeared to have months to live, [but] were then unable to return quickly enough" to spend quality time with their dying loved one (Munshi et al., 2020; Najeeb, 2020). Hospital administrators need to recognize that family members are not offered any level of reassurance when "a hospital team member [sits] with their loved one during the dying process [if staffing even allows]" in order to prevent patients from spending their last moments of life fully alone (Leiter & Gelfand, 2021). This multi-stakeholder situation becomes especially upsetting, frustrating, and stressful when staff do not speak the same language as patients, which creates barriers in effective communication, proper advocacy of patient needs, respect for the grieving process, and expressing love or forgiveness to loved ones (Kuntz et al., 2020). As a result, healthcare workers have "reported substantial distress associated with being a 'placeholder' for families at the end of life" (Munshi et al., 2020; Najeeb, 2020). Visitation restrictions that have forced many patients to die in isolation and separated from loved ones is psychologically and emotionally distressing and confusing for patients, family members, and healthcare teams, resulting in an urgent need for public health authorities to renegotiate family presence policies.

For compounding reasons, including a need to prevent emotionally overburdening clinicians, experts in quality, safety, and infectious disease must work with patient-family advocates in order to develop stronger person-centered guidelines that will help hospitals preserve family presence. Assessing and comparing risk between each of the different approaches to visitor policies is difficult to do because direct comparisons cannot be made, but it is clear that we have a duty to prevent the psycho-morbidity that arises when family presence is prohibited at the bedside (Downar & Kekewich, 2021; Leiter & Gelfand, 2021). When exceptions were made for brief visits from one or two family members at the very end of a patient's life, this usually only applied to "patients who decided to transition to comfort-focused care and, in many cases, stop life support" (Leiter & Gelfand, 2021). If hospitals allow families to visit "only if their loved one transitioned away from life-sustaining measures, [then] rather than helping families say goodbye, [a visitation exception becomes] a form of coercion" (Leiter & Gelfand, 2021). Moreover, by only allowing two visitors to stay at the bedside, families are faced with making incredibly difficult choices about who can share final goodbyes and last moments with a loved one, and hospital staff who have to comply with these rules are forced to play a role in causing pain and distress that can last a lifetime.

Not only did healthcare workers experience intense moral distress over having to enforce these policies, but they also have to consider the ways in which these regulations deeply conflict with a clinician's ability to uphold the principles of person-centered care and provide patients and families with just and humane care. After witnessing the preventable pain and suffering caused by family separation in acute care and palliative care settings, many healthcare workers support reinstating "safe, compassionate family presence policies within communities...during [these] challenging circumstances [with COVID-19, especially because they wish to honor" the essential role that family care partners play as members of the care team" (Frampton et al., 2020). Families have to be recognized as part of the standard of care in hospital settings, not viewed as indulgences that can and should be forsaken during public health crises, when their role as care partners actually needs to be regarded with an even greater level of importance. Rightful acknowledgement of the important role families play in clinical settings is a must, even and especially during a pandemic, when clinicians are already overworked and should not be made to feel responsible for enforcing policies that cause patients and families to experience direct harm and intense suffering (Selman et al., 2020). Implementing these humane visitation guidelines will allow clinicians to not only build greater levels of trust with the patients and families they serve, but will also help healthcare workers relieve the tension they feel, promote shared decision-making, and respect the rights of patients and family care partners. By using a well-designed plan and carefully instructing families on how to safely and properly use PPE, hospitals would be able to safely allow family presence at the bedside for sick and dying patients during this pandemic.

Balancing Person-Centered Care and Contagion Control

As local and national public health authorities and hospital administrators work to reintegrate compassionate end-of-life visits for sick and dying loved ones, they must work to limit the spread of COVID-19, especially for hospitals in communities with an already rising prevalence of disease. Respecting family members as care partners in clinical settings is necessary, but increasing visitation will create some difficulties in maintaining adequate physical distancing protocol, particularly near elevators and entrances (Johns Hopkins Medicine, 2020). Although visitation restrictions might appear to be an effective way to "[limit] the number of visitors allowed at one time [and] reduce how many people get exposed to the risk of infection," research has demonstrated that problems with transmission are not resolved with these policies (Downar & Kekewich, 2021). Family members living in one household often visit sick and dying loved ones in the hospital by "cycling between being at the bedside and being outside the hospital multiple times in a single day" (Downar & Kekewich, 2021). As family members switch out and take turns visiting, they engage in "the removal of personal protective equipment and transit within the hospital [which] is likely to increase the risk of transmission substantially more than simply allowing all visitors to remain at the bedside for the duration of their visit...space permitting" (Downar & Kekewich, 2021). Ultimately, policies that place morally distressing visitor limits at the bedside of sick and dying patients do not truly serve to effectively reduce the chances of COVID-19 transmission between family members, hospital staff, or other patients.

Hospitals must move away from implementing a straightforward "no visitation, no exceptions" policy that must be adhered to at all times and instead focus on using a combination of transparent, evidence-based standards for visitor policies that are tied to rates of viral spread and rigorous use of infection prevention and control (IPAC) measures. Appropriately responding to COVID-19 and reducing the risk of transmission while promoting whole-person welfare can be achieved by: (1) continually reassessing "whether there is a need for restrictions based on current factual evidence" and CDC guidance; (2) minimizing risk of physical presence by following appropriate infection control and prevention guidelines; (3) communicating proactively so that there is transparency about facility policies on PPE use and compliance; (4) using a "shared decision-making approach to communicate risks and benefits in cases where family can be physically" at the bedside; and (5) enlisting "family as members of the care team" who have a duty to follow safety protocols (Frampton et al., 2020). With this plan, there essentially should be no limit on care partners if space allows and the administrators in specific clinical settings believe that it would be safe and feasible, and even in circumstances with the greatest visitation risk level, family members could be cautiously offered compassionate exceptions to restrictions (Johns Hopkins Medicine, 2020).

When our society is inevitably faced with the problem of future global health emergencies, it is imperative that pandemic preparedness plans become centered around flexible guidelines that are not only based on rates of viral spread and visitation risk levels that assess the number of outbreak cases in the community, but also informed by state and county public health information as well as hospital conditions in order to protect patients, relatives/care partners, healthcare teams, and the broader public. While most nosocomial outbreaks originate from "asymptomatic healthcare workers...using shared [community] spaces for breaks and meals," a small percentage of transmission has been caused by asymptomatic visitors who lacked "sufficient education in PPE use or who did not articulate symptoms on entry screening" (Munshi et al., 2020). Therefore, in order to safely preserve family presence, visitors must not only accurately and honestly report their symptoms, but they must also be educated in the effective and appropriate use of and compliance with PPE, which is a process that may require additional staffing (Munshi et al., 2020; Seibert et al., 2018). Ultimately, visitation should be monitored to ensure that (1) facilities are screening visitors for the ability to comply with precautions; (2) facilities have enough staff to provide instruction to visitors on hand hygiene, limiting surfaces touched, and appropriate use of PPE while on the premises; (3) visitors understand the need to leave patient rooms during procedures that might generate or spread viral aerosols; and (4) visitors are instructed to only visit the patient room and avoid going to other locations in the facility (Seibert et al., 2017; Johns Hopkins Medicine, 2020). The safety and well-being of healthcare workers, patients, and family visitors/care partners must be protected, and with collaborative efforts and compassionate leadership, visitation policies can be made safer, less restricted, and more equitable.

Conclusion

The rigid and uncompromising visitor restrictions put in place by many hospitals and healthcare facilities at the start of the pandemic were reasonable precautions used to limit the spread of a dangerous and poorly understood pathogen. However, now that we have been operating with more than three years of experience dealing with the novel coronavirus and have greater understanding of benefits from proper PPE use and monitoring, healthcare facilities must be urged to adopt new end-of-life visitor policies that respect the psychosocial needs of family members and patients without causing a substantially increased risk of viral transmission. Based on findings discussed throughout this paper, I believe it would be unreasonable to continue operating with complete visitation restrictions in hospitals, especially in end-of-life contexts, where such policies do more harm than good. As public health experts reexamine the safety guidelines used in hospital settings, the threat of global health emergencies must be considered within the context of other threats to health and well-being, such as the unsupported loss of loved ones and compounding grief, which have complex and long-term consequences. The perspectives and voices of patients and families must be strongly regarded in order to promote trust in medical and public health authorities as well as develop policies that are based in scientific justification and compassion. Although we have implemented tools that have helped us become better prepared for managing pandemics, we have failed to address the collective trauma that arises when families are separated from dying loved ones. Moving forward, visitation policies have to proactively respond to emerging public health crises and emergencies while still operating from a person-centered approach. Unless healthcare authorities take action to reconstruct the system and hospital policies designed to safeguard communities against infectious disease outbreaks, patients will continue to spend their last moments of life isolated from their loved ones, and the failure of medical institutions to address this dire problem will be a defining memory of this pandemic.

Acknowledgements

The author is thankful for the phenomenal guidance and mentorship she received in the theory and practice of clinical ethics from Dr. Mark Aulisio and Ms. Elise Ellick from the Department of Bioethics at Case Western Reserve University. Their endless support has been invaluable and has nurtured the development of a compassion-driven perspective in bioethics. The author thanks Ying Xiong for his efforts in revising this paper from the time it was written to its publication in order to better reflect a timeless message of continually reinvestigating the whys behind our work, beliefs, and values, especially when they impact the lives of those surrounding us. The author is further appreciative of her parents, Dr. Young Chung and Mrs. Cindy Chung, for inspiring each of their children to be the change they want to see in the world and for leading by example. This paper was written in beloved memory and honor of the author's dear grandfather, Hak Chung.

Works Cited

Azoulay E, Cariou A, Bruneel F, et al. (2020). Symptoms of anxiety, depression and peritraumatic dissociation in critical care clinicians managing COVID-19 patients: a cross-sectional study. *Am J Respir Crit Care Med*, 202, 1388–1398.

Downar J & Kekewich M. (2021). Improving family access to dying patients during the COVID-19 pandemic. *The Lancet Respiratory Medicine*. Retrieved on February 1, 2021 from https://www.thelancet.com/journals/lanres/article/PIIS2213-2600(21)00025-4/fulltext.

Frampton S, Agrawal S, Guastello S. (2020). Guidelines for Family Presence Policies During the COVID-19 Pandemic. *JAMA Health Forum*. Retrieved on February 1, 2021 from https://jamanetwork.com/channels/health-forum/fullarticle/2768108.

Goldfarb MJ, Bibas L, Bartlett V, et al. (2017). Outcomes of patient-and family-centred care interventions in the ICU: a systematic review and meta-analysis. *Crit Care Med* 45, 1751–1761.

Helms J, Kremer S, Merdji H, et al. (2020). Delirium and encephalopathy in severe COVID-19: a cohort analysis of ICU patients. *Crit Care* 24, 491.

Hurst H, Griffiths J, Hunt C, et al. (2019). A realist evaluation of the implementation of open visiting in an acute care setting for older people. *BMC Health Serv Res* 19, 867.

Johns Hopkins Medicine. (2020). Visitor Guidelines for Patient Care Partners During COVID-19. The Johns Hopkins University. Retrieved on February 1, 2021 from https://www.hopkinsmedicine.org/coronavirus/visitor-guidelines.html.

Kuntz JG, Kavalieratos D, Esper G, et al. (2020). Feasibility and acceptability of inpatient palliative care e-family meetings during COVID-19 pandemic. *J Pain Sym Man* 60, 28.

Leiter RE & Gelfand S. (2021). Even during a pandemic, hospitals must make family visits and communication the standard of care. STAT News. Retrieved on February 1, 2021 from https://www.statnews.com/2021/01/09/even-during-a-pandemic-hospitals-must-make-family-visits-and-communication-the-standard-of-care/.

Mayland CR, Harding AJE, Preston N, & Payne S. (2020). Supporting adults bereaved through COVID-19: a rapid review of the impact of previous pandemics on grief and bereavement. *J Pain Sym Man* 60, 33–39.

Munshi L, Evans G, & Razak F. (2020). The case for relaxing no-visitor policies in hospitals during the ongoing COVID-19 pandemic. *CMAJ* 193(4), 135–137.

Najeeb U. (2020). COVID-19 reflections: Phone call [blog]. *CMAJ*. Retrieved on February 1, 2021 from http://cmajblogs.com/phone-call/.

Nassar AP, Besen B, Robinson CC, et al. (2018). Flexible versus restrictive visiting policies in ICUs: a systematic review and meta-analysis. *Crit Care Med* 46, 1175–1180.

Otani H, Yoshida S, Morita T, et al. (2017). Meaningful communication before death, but not present at the time of death itself, is associated with better outcomes on measures of depression and complicated grief among bereaved family members of cancer patients. *J Pain Sym Man* 54, 273–279.

Salgado CD, Farr BM, Hall KK, et al. (2002). Influenza in the acute hospital setting. *Lancet Infect Dis* 2, 145–155.

Seibert G, Ewers T, Barker A, et al. (2018). What do visitors know and how do they feel about contact precautions? *Am J Infect Control* 46, 115–117.

Selman LE, Chao D, Sowden R, et al. (2020). Bereavement support on the frontline of COVID-19: recommendations for hospital clinicians. *J Pain Sym Man* 60, 81–86.

Ting R, Edmonds P, Higginson I J, Sleeman K E. (2020). Palliative care for patients with severe COVID-19, 370(2710), 1.

Zeh RD, Santry H, Monsour C, et al. (2020). Impact of visitor restriction rules on the postoperative experience of COVID-19 negative patients undergoing surgery. *Surgery* 168, 770–776.

Zhou Q, Gao Y, Wang X, et al. (2020). Nosocomial infections among patients with COVID-19, SARS and MERS: a rapid review and meta-analysis. *Ann Transl Med* 8, 629.

Moral Courage
When the "Line in the Sand" Demands a Response

Nikki Coleman

On October 1, 2020, the Australian Defence Force (ADF) launched a single set of Defence Values as a part of the Chief of Defence Force's cultural reform process, *Pathway to Change 2017–2022*. These values are:[1]

- Service: the selflessness of character to place the security and interests of our nation and its people ahead of my own
- Courage: the strength of character to say and do the right thing, always, especially in the face of adversity
- Respect: the humanity of character to value others and treat them with dignity
- Integrity: the consistency of character to align my thoughts, words, and actions to do what is right
- Excellence: the willingness of character to strive each day to be the best I can be, both professionally and personally

All members of the ADF, including civilians working in the Australian Public Service (APS), are expected to abide by and live up to these values. What this means in practice is that the values are discussed regularly from the highest ranks of the ADF down to the lowest, through forums such as the ADF annual report to the CO's hour on bases and ships. Even the Religious Advisory Committee to the Services (RACS) have created an in-depth guide for all ADF members on Defence values and behaviours. This document puts forward the Buddhist, Christian, Hindu, Islamic, Jewish, and Sikh responses to Defence values in order to encourage ADF members of faith to align their own personal religious values with that of the Defence Values.[2] The Defence values are displayed prominently in most ADF buildings and ships, and additionally are often used to hold all ADF members accountable for their actions in disciplinary matters.

---

1. "Our Values. Defence: Overview," Department of Defence, accessed 30 July 2022, https://www.defence.gov.au/about/at-a-glance.
2. "RACS Response to Defence Values," Religious Advisory Committee to the Services, 2021.

The ADF does not just talk about courage as a value, it also awards decorations (medals), commendations, and unit citations for outstanding heroic courage in action—the highest of these decorations being the Victoria Cross. The Victoria Cross is Australia's highest military honour, granted sparingly for "the most conspicuous gallantry, or daring or pre-eminent acts of valour or self-sacrifice or extreme devotion to duty in the presence of the enemy."[3] It is vitally important that these acts of self-sacrifice and courage are recognised in this way. However, it does raise the question of why only acts of physical courage are recognised and rewarded. Currently Australia does not have a specific award or decoration to recognise moral courage. Where a member of the ADF has had the "strength of character to say and do the right thing in the face of adversity," we do not recognise or reward that Defence member for their moral courage.[4] This then raises the question—Why, as an institution, does the ADF have courage as a core value—especially since in the ADF values statement it is by definition moral courage that we should all aspire to—if we do not actually value it enough to recognise and reward moral courage? I will discuss this further later on in my paper, but for now, let us turn our attention to the question of "What is moral courage?"

What is moral courage?

In *On War*, Clausewitz argued that there are two kinds of courage—physical courage and moral courage—but that both are vitally important in war.[5] As Clausewitz states, some actions will be examples of both physical and moral courage, which in turn makes it difficult to separate the two at times. The actions of those protecting civilians at the Mỹ Lai massacre are an example of both moral courage (standing up to their own troops who were raping and killing unarmed civilians) and physical courage (putting their physical safety at risk in order to save the civilians from being killed).[6] Whilst some situations make it difficult to separate physical and moral courage, there are examples of courage which is either physical or moral courage in nature.

---

3. "Gallantry Decorations," The Governor General of the Commonwealth of Australia, accessed 31 July 2022, https://www.gg.gov.au/australian-honours-and-awards/gallantry-decorations.
4. Department of Defence, "Our Values: Overview."
5. Carl von Clausewitz, *On War*, Book 1, Chapter 3, accessed 23 August 2022, www.clausewitz.com/readings/OnWar1873/BK1ch03.html.
6. Hugh Thompson, "The Heroes of My Lai. Hugh Thompson," University of Missouri-Kansas City, accessed 05 September 2016, http://law2.umkc.edu/faculty/projects/ftrials/mylai/Myl_hero.html#RON.

In her chapter on courage in *Military Virtues,* Pauline Shanks Kaurin argues that physical courage in the military is often seen as the "courage of the warrior," where a person risks their own physical safety to win a military objective or rescue those in peril.[7] In the ADF, we recognise this physical courage through various awards and gallantry decorations for heroic courage in action. An example of this was the awarding of the Victoria Cross to Trooper Mark Donaldson in 2009 for his rescue of an interpreter whilst under heavy enemy fire.[8] In the civilian sphere, we also recognise and reward physical courage through the Australian Bravery Decorations.[9] These acts of physical courage by our military members and those in the community should absolutely be recognised and rewarded. They remind us of the lengths that ordinary people placed in extraordinary circumstances will go to in order to rescue or protect vulnerable people and to protect Australia and its interests. The process for awarding these decorations is long and thorough, beginning in Defence with nominations from the chain of command, as well as a thorough investigation into whether both the recipient and the actions nominated are worthy of recognition, especially when it is Australia's highest decoration, the Victoria Cross. Thus, a significant number of resources are put towards examining acts of physical courage by ADF members. If the ADF truly wants its members to stand up and do the right thing, I would argue that we need to be more proactive in recognising those who have shown extraordinary moral courage at great risk and cost to themselves. Being intentional about encouraging, recognising, and rewarding moral courage would potentially require similar resources being allocated as are currently allocated to the recognition of physical courage.

One barrier to rewarding moral courage is that it has the potential to accidentally expose those who have not shown moral courage themselves. This tension around moral courage places a pressure on those in command as they balance these tensions between recognising their subordinates for displaying outstanding moral courage against the potential of highlighting the lack of moral courage of others involved in the same situation if they were aware of the unacceptable behaviour and did not take action against it. If a commander then recognises a member for their moral courage in

---

7. Pauline Shanks Kaurin, "Courage: Overview" in *Military Virtues,* ed Michael Skerker et al, (Havant, UK: Howgate Publishing, 2019), 104.
8. "Act of Gallantry, Trooper Mark Donaldson VC," Department of Prime Minister and Cabinet, accessed 23 August 2022, www.pmc.gov.au/act-gallantry.
9. "Australian Bravery Decorations," Governor General of Australia, accessed 23 August 2022, www.gg.gov.au/australian-honours-and-awards/australian-bravery-decorations.

calling out unacceptable behaviour, it additionally puts more senior members in the awkward position of having to answer questions over their own handling of the situation. This highlights the unusual situation where if an organisation does not genuinely value moral courage, the act of *rewarding* moral courage becomes an act of moral courage in itself.

This fraught situation creates a dissonance between the promotion of moral courage through values statements and cultural reform programs, whilst morally courageous behaviour may be overlooked or requires an act of moral courage itself to reward such behaviour. This situation does not set up an organisation to succeed in promoting moral courage of its members or bring about change through cultural reform programs. When leaders must risk their careers to reward examples of exemplary moral courage, we are further compounding injustices in situations where acts of moral courage could have prevented the harm that unacceptable or illegal behaviour brings about.

Additionally, if leaders turn a blind eye to or even cover up these poor behaviours, all those working with and under them notice it. This is further compounded when commanders are at the same time calling on their subordinates to show moral courage and "do the right thing."[10] This dissonance between words and actions undermines the moral authority of military organisations, which has far-reaching implications on the organisation to provide vital capability. Unfortunately this gap between words and actions regarding moral courage (and integrity) also leads to experienced and capable military members leaving their service because they feel that they can no longer work in an organisation which promotes one thing (by including courage in values statements and codes of behaviour), but then acts contrary to that value.[11] This drain from the organisation of highly principled military members significantly impacts the culture of a military organisation, as well as the capability provided by those members, which ultimately has a negative impact on national security.

There is a spectrum of situations that will demand moral courage. For some, the "line in the sand" will be speaking up when seeing unacceptable behaviour in the form of bullying or sexual harassment. For others, it will be a moment when they have to show moral courage to save the lives of others.

---

10. The official ADF policy is that there is zero tolerance to unacceptable behaviour. However, numerous submissions to the Royal Commission show that this is not happening in every case, with particular concerns regarding sexual harassment and sexual assault cases.
11. The value of courage and integrity are closely linked. However, I will not be examining integrity in this paper due to space constraints.

Probably the most famous example of this extreme impact of moral courage is when helicopter pilot Warrant Officer Hugh Thompson and his flight crew intervened in the Mỹ Lai massacre in 1968. Through their selfless and repeated actions of placing themselves between US troops and unarmed civilians, they showed enormous physical and moral courage.[12] After the massacre, Warrant Officer Thompson was placed under enormous pressure to assist in the multiple cover-ups of the events of that day and was threatened with disciplinary action for turning his weapons on American soldiers.[13] Instead of being rewarded for showing moral and physical courage in stopping the slaughter and rape of innocent civilians, Thompson was ostracised by his peers, vilified by the public, and even received death threats long after he had left the military.[14] It was only in 1998, after a long letter-writing campaign by Professor David Egan and others, that Warrant Officer Thompson and the fellow members of his helicopter crew were recognised for their moral courage at Mỹ Lai with the Soldiers Medal award. The actions of Warrant Officer Hugh Thompson and his flight crew on that day are a shining example of moral courage at great personal cost to themselves.

In 2013, then Chief of Army Lt. Gen. David Morrison released a video to all members of the Australian Army which quickly went public and spread virally around the world.[15] In this video and in subsequent speeches, Lt. Gen. Morrison was speaking out against the abhorrent behaviour of some army members towards women, behaviour which he described as "explicit, derogatory, demeaning and repugnant."[16] As a female military ethicist based at the Australian Defence Force Academy in Canberra, I received dozens of emails from colleagues all around the world commenting on the video. There are

---

12. Hugh Thompson, "The Heroes of My Lai. Hugh Thompson." University of Missouri-Kansas City, accessed 05 September 2016, http://law2.umkc.edu/faculty/projects/ftrials/mylai/Myl_hero.html#RON.
13. "Obituary: Hugh Thompson Jr., My Lai rescuer, dies at 62," *The New York Times*, 06 January 2006, https://www.nytimes.com/2006/01/06/world/americas/obituary-hugh-thompson-jr-my-lai-rescuer-dies-at-62.html.
14. Hugh Thompson, "Moral Courage in Combat: The My Lai Story: Lecture," United States Naval Academy. Annapolis MD: U.S. Naval Academy Center for the Study of Professional Military Ethics, accessed 22 August 2022, https://www.usna.edu/Ethics/publications/documents/ThompsonPg1-28_Final.pdf
15. *Everyone Matters*," Australian Chief to Sexist Soldiers: Respect Women or GET OUT," YouTube video, accessed 23 August 2022, https://www.youtube.com/watch?v=dRQBtDtZTGA (unfortunately the official Australian Army YouTube account no longer has the video of Lt. Gen. Morrison available online).
16. "Australian military investigates 'explicit emails,'" *BBC News Service*, accessed 23 August 2022 https://www.bbc.com/news/world-asia-22885465.

many interesting moments in the video, but seeing a visibly angry Chief of Army, who was vibrating with rage as he told those who can't get behind an inclusive army to "get out," was especially memorable.[17] Lt. Gen. Morrison encouraged soldiers to "show moral courage and take a stand" against unacceptable behaviour, stating that he would "be ruthless in ridding the army of people who cannot live up to its values."[18] However, the most famous line from the video was "the standard you walk past is the standard you accept."[19]

From Lt. Gen. Morrison's approach it was clear that this was a turning point for how unacceptable behaviour would be handled in the Australian Army and the wider Australian Defence Force. "The Standard You Walk Past is the Standard You Accept" became famous for encouraging good bystander (or upstander) behaviour. For years after this video aired, every military ethics conference I attended had at least one presentation use this phrase and talk about it as a turning point in for women in military organisations all over the world.[20] I have seen it on bumper stickers, T-shirts, and email signatures all around the world.

While I am very proud to be part of the Australian Defence Force, which has had such a high-ranking leader as Lt. Gen. Morrison speak out forcefully against unacceptable behaviour, I wish there had been more advances in stamping out unacceptable behaviour in the ADF.[21] Instead of the ADF having a reputation for how well we deal with sexual assaults, sexual harassment and bullying, we are unfortunately currently being named by victims as an organisation who covers up these behaviours.[22,23] Sadly, those who show moral courage and speak out against these unacceptable behaviours are often seen to be the problem instead of those who perpetrate and/or cover up the abuse. Despite the official policy that victims and impacted units are to be advised of outcomes, some feel the system is used

---

17. Ibid.
18. Ibid.
19. Ibid.
20. Ibid.
21. Tom Stayner, "Sexual Assault Complaints in Australian Defence Force Soar to Eight-year High," *SBS News*, 22 October 2021, www.sbs.com.au/news/article/sexual-assault-complaints-in-australian-defence-force-soar-to-eight-year-high/dqdhwuknv.
22. "Uniform Justice: Telegraph campaign to end defence abuse of women," *Daily Telegraph*, 7 May 2022, https://www.dailytelegraph.com.au/news/nsw/uniform-justice-telegraph-campaign-to-end-defence-abuse-of-women/.
23. Harley Dennet, "ADF Victims of sexual assault rising, not told of military justice outcomes: report, *The Canberra Times*, 29 March 2022, https://www.canberratimes.com.au/story/7676819/defence-chiefs-warned-of-rising-sexual-misconduct-as-victims-lose-faith/.

to protect the abusers; at the very least there is the perception that this is the case, because victims and impacted members are not told of military actions against those found guilty of abuse.[24]

This lack of "transparency of management of outcomes" was found by Professor Pru Goward to be of concern in her IGADF inquiry into handling of sexual misconduct in the ADF.[25] She additionally found that the "increase in the use of administrative action to address sexual misconduct" rather than the use of the Defence Force Discipline Act, limited the "transparency of management outcomes" leading to Commanding Officers struggling "between the competing principles of privacy and closure for victims in providing advice to victims on the outcome of their sexual misconduct complaints."[26] This may be why Professor Goward found that the majority of victims who gave feedback to the IGADF inquiry "considered the process had been unfair and unsupportive."[27]

Despite these concerning findings by Professor Goward, it must be noted that the ADF has made a sustained and determined effort over the past ten years to change the culture within defence around the problem of sexual misconduct. This work has led to large improvements in the rate of sexual misconduct in the ADF identified through anonymous surveys, with the ADF currently sitting around 5.7% compared to the civilian rate of 20% in civilian workplaces.[28] Additionally research by Professor Pru Goward and the IGADF found in comparison to civilian organisations "the ADF is quicker to finalise sexual offences and fewer complaints are withdrawn than in the civilian criminal system."[29]

While I am glad that Lt. Gen. Morrison decided to act in the case of the "Jedi Council" sex scandal, where ADF members were distributing explicit and degrading images of women via email, there are accounts that this happened only after the media became involved.[30] Because of the leader

---

24. Ibid.
25. Inspector General of the ADF, "Own-Initiative Inquiry. Implementation of Military Justice Arrangements for Dealing With Sexual Misconduct in the Australian Defence Force," 21 November 2021, https://www.defence.gov.au/sites/default/files/2022-03/IGADF-Report.pdf
26. Ibid. Finding 10, Finding 15.
27. Ibid. Executive Summary, paragraph 15.
28. Ibid. Executive Summary, paragraph 5.
29. Ibid. Finding 9.
30. Ross Eastgate, "David Morrison must take responsibility over army sexual abuse allegations and resign as Australian of the Year," *The Courier Mail*, 7 Feb 2016, www.couriermail.com.au/news/opinion/david-morrison-must-take-responsibility-over-army-sexual-abuse-allegations-and-resign-as-australian-of-the-year/news-story/30968c74c32ae58a1dfd694905851a8f.

that Lt. Gen. Morrison has shown himself to be, I am sure that the delay in the handling of the "Jedi Council" scandal and subsequent video was not because of a lack of concern for the victims, but rather is a symptom of the current opacity of ADF processes in regards to issues of this kind. Such an occurrence by military members speaking out to the media is rare because it is illegal for ADF members to speak to the media. This can then lead to the situation where there is no genuine appetite to change the unofficial culture of "covering things up," as there is no effective external oversight of how the ADF handles problematic or abusive behaviours.[31]

Regarding courage of all forms, there needs to be a balance for both physical and moral courage. Too much physical courage can make a military member reckless and put their life and those of their squad mates at unnecessary risk. Too little physical courage is a form of cowardice and likewise puts a member's squad mates at further risk, as they cannot rely upon the member to have their back. As with physical courage, there also needs to be a balance in regards to moral courage. A potential example of too much moral courage would be the acts of Julian Assange, who claims to be holding military actions to account, but has done it in such a way as to endanger countless people through his actions by revealing the identity of undercover operatives to our enemies. Conversely, turning a blind eye to sexual harassment in the workplace is an example of too little moral courage, as perpetrators may be emboldened or even accidentally encouraged to move on to more serious acts of sexual assault, clearly increasing the harm to the victims. One way of judging if we have achieved the right balance for the extremes of courage is to look at the harm the actions place upon others—particularly those who are vulnerable and in need of extra protection. If our actions harm others who require protection, then the balance required for acts of courage is wrong.

When teaching a class at the Australian Defence College a few years ago a student made the insightful comment about moral courage that as Defence members "we would happily fall on a grenade and lose our life to save a mate on the battlefield, but we wouldn't risk our career by standing up and doing the right thing and showing moral courage." That comment

---

31. "Uniform Justice: Telegraph campaign to end defence abuse of women," *Daily Telegraph*, 07 May 2022, https://www.dailytelegraph.com.au/news/nsw/uniform-justice-telegraph-campaign-to-end-defence-abuse-of-women/. For further information on this concept, please see my previous research on this topic https://unsworks.unsw.edu.au/handle/1959.4/58006.

highlighted for me a problem with moral courage in military organisations. If our soldiers, sailors and aviators die as a result of showing physical courage they are given a warrior's funeral and their family is looked after by the ADF, the Department of Veterans' Affairs (DVA), Legacy and numerous other ex-service organisations. It is truly horrible that they have died, but they are seen to have made the ultimate sacrifice and we see their actions as noble. On the other hand, if a Defence member shows moral courage by standing up against wrongful behaviour perpetrated by their peers, or worse, by their chain of command, then they are often ostracised, punished, and bullied. It costs the individual dearly in terms of career (promotions and deployments are rarely given to those perceived to be "troublemakers"), health, including mental health, and strained or fractured relationships.[32]

If our leaders demand moral courage from soldiers, sailors and aviators but do not recognise or reward it and if those who show moral courage are instead punished or left to protect themselves from those whose actions are anathema to Defence values, then this sends a very clear message that although moral courage is in our list of values, it is not meaningfully valued. This tension between words and actions also sends the message that showing moral courage just is not worth the personal cost, especially if everyone around you and above you is looking the other way.

What happens when individuals fail to show moral courage?

When individuals fail to show moral courage, and thus do not stand up and do the right thing, they have an increased risk of mental health issues including depression, anxiety, post traumatic stress disorder and moral injury. Much has been written in recent years on moral injury, so I will not go over it here, however I wish to highlight that research on moral injury has found that the impact of "perpetrating, failing to prevent, bearing witness to, or learning about acts that transgress deeply held moral beliefs and expectations" (i.e. much of what we would define as a failure of moral courage), have a "lasting psychological, biological, spiritual, behavioural, and social impact."[33,34,35] In this way we can see that when individuals fail

---

32. Adavies. "Whistleblower waits for apology," 12 March 2012, www.couriermail.com.au/news/whistleblower-waits-for-apology/news-story/d6a536b0cc7018e2e5b8bd229a4b2815.
33. Timothy Hodgson, and Lindsay Carey. "Moral Injury and Definitional Clarity: Betrayal, Spirituality and the Role of Chaplains," *Journal of Religion and Health* 56, no. 4 (2017): 1212–1228.
34. Nikki Coleman, "Moral Status and the Re-Integration Process,." in *Moral Injury: Unseen Wounds in an Age of Barbarism*, ed. Tom Frame (Sydney: UNSW Press, 2015), pp. 205–219.
35. Brett Litz, et al., "Moral Injury and Moral Repair in War Veterans: A Preliminary

to show moral courage, they increase the chance of negative mental health outcomes (including moral injury), for themselves, those they work with and for those they command.

When individuals fail to show moral courage, it can also undermine the moral reputation of a whole unit or even whole military organisation. In 2019 an Australian Navy Exchange Officer was convicted in Australia of "abusing his public office," for his role in the Fat Leonard scandal whilst posted as an exchange officer with the US Navy's 7th Fleet.[36] The Fat Leonard situation was an example of endemic corruption, which occurred when senior naval officers in the 7th Fleet were among other things passing classified operational information to the logistics company Glenn Defense Marine Asia and in particular to the CEO of GDMA Leonard Glenn Francis (known widely as Fat Leonard).[37] This information was passed along in return for bribes of money, luxury gifts, prostitutes and lavish parties. The Fat Leonard scandal has been named as "perhaps the worse national-security breach of its kind to hit the Navy since the end of the Cold War" because of the impact of the release of classified operational material to a civilian contractor with no need to receive the information.[38] In 2008 the Australian Exchange Officer was posted to the 7th Fleet as Australia's Navy liaison officer and soon became aware of another US Navy officer leaking information to Fat Leonard. Instead of reporting this breach to his US and Australian chains of command, this exchange officer was recruited to also provide classified information, even going as far as creating a fake email address to get around US Navy computer system firewalls. The actions of naval officers such as this exchange officer and the dozens more US Navy officers involved cast a shadow on the reputation of thousands of US Naval officers, and that of both the 7th Fleet and the US Navy as a whole.

Whilst it is easy to apportion blame to the individual officers for not doing the right thing, if the culture within the US Navy's 7th fleet, or even within the ADF, had been one where the moral courage for calling out wrongful behaviour was rewarded, then this situation of widespread cor-

---

Model and Intervention Strategy," *Clinical Psychology Review* 29, no. 8 (December 2009): 700, 697.

36. Alexandra Back, "Fat Leonard scandal: Australian Navy lieutenant commander avoids jail," *The Canberra Times*, 14 Feb. 2019, www.canberratimes.com.au/story/5995232/fat-leonard-scandal-australian-navy-lieutenant-commander-avoids-jail.

37. Cid Standifer, "Timeline: Fat Leonard Case," U.S. Naval Institute, 16 Mar. 2017, https://news.usni.org/2017/03/16/timeline-fat-leonard-case.

38. Craig Whitlock, "The man who seduced the 7th Fleet," *The Washington Post*, 27 May, 2016, www.washingtonpost.com/sf/investigative/2016/05/27/the-man-who-seduced-the-7th-fleet/.

ruption would probably not have been able to grow to the size that it did. Individual rogue military members taking bribes and passing on classified sensitive information is much more easily identified and stamped out when the prevailing culture is that of encouraging, recognising and rewarding those who show moral courage by being upstanding against such blatantly illegal behaviour. Imagine if instead of initially feeling pressured to turn a blind eye to the Fat Leonard scheme, the Australian exchange officer had known that if they called out such corruption that they would be supported by their chain of command in the U.S. Fleet and Royal Australian Navy. If Australia had a way of encouraging, recognising and rewarding such outstanding moral courage, we would be praising the upstanding behaviour of the exchange officer as an example of a military member living up to the value of courage (as well as that of integrity) rather than being embarrassed by the actions of an exchange officer.

While individual actions can impact negatively on the reputation of an organisation, when individuals stand up and show moral courage it can encourage others to step forward and show moral courage themselves. A recent example of this is the public testimony of White House aide Cassidy Hutchinson. Her testimony before the United States Select Committee on the January 6 Attack inspired other more senior White House staff to come forward and give private testimony to the committee.[39] In the face of enormous public vitriol towards her personally, Cassidy Hutchinson's steps to tell the truth about what happened on 6 January 2020 were a shining example of moral courage, especially since it came at enormous cost to herself.

Another example of an individual showing enormous moral courage which brought about profound change, was the actions Captain Ian Fishback (later promoted to Major). Whilst stationed in Iraq with the US Army, Fishback tried to raise concerns regarding the treatment of detainees with his chain of command, but was largely ignored for more than seventeen months. Eventually in 2005, Fishback wrote to Senator John McCain which led to anti-torture legislation, the Detainee Treatment Act, bringing about a dramatic change in the way in which detainees were treated in Iraq and elsewhere.[40] The actions of individuals such as Cassidy Hutchinson and Ian Fishback in speaking up for the truth should be commended as brave acts

---

39. Robert Draper, "Cassidey Hutchinson: Why the Jan. 6 Committee Rushed Her Testimony," *The New York Times*, 10 July 2022, https://www.nytimes.com/2022/07/10/us/politics/cassidy-hutchinson-jan-6-testimony.html.
40. Ian Fishback, "A Matter of Honor," *The Washington Post*, 28 Sept. 2005, https://www.washingtonpost.com/wp-dyn/content/article/2005/09/27/AR2005092701527.html

of moral courage at enormous personal cost, but should also not be necessary if more people working alongside them also showed moral courage to speak up when behaviours and situations are unacceptable.

What happens when organisations fail to show moral courage?

When military organisations fail to show moral courage, it has a profound impact on individual military members. In particular, the unfortunate practice of covering up sexual abuse in military organisations has a significant impact on a large number of military women and men.[41] One member who contacted me when they heard I was writing this paper stated: "For me, the assaults were less painful than the cover-ups and how people treated me."[42] The covering up of abuse whilst problematic on its own, also leads to the victim being ostracised by their peers, compounding the harm done by the original perpetrator. This situation could be reduced and potentially eliminated if military organisations adopted more transparent and robust processes for dealing with unacceptable behaviour and abuse, and more robust systems for removing from the military those found guilty of these actions. The common use of "admin action" by commanders to deal with those found guilty of unacceptable behaviour and abuse leads to the situation where outcomes against perpetrators are neither transparent nor consistent and can potentially be used to cover up unacceptable behaviour. This situation has been noted in the research by James Connor and Ben Wadham, who found that "the effects of a closed system that perpetuates administrative violence against members can be a contributing factor in veterans self-harming" and that administrative processes are "used to further traumatise victimised members … (creating a) second assault."[43]

From a military ethics perspective what is even worse than the cover-up of abuse is when the perpetrators are not held accountable for their actions in any meaningful way and are subsequently promoted to positions of authority.[44] Whilst it is shocking enough to have someone who has been

---

41. Ian Austen, "Canada's Military, Where Sexual Misconduct Went to the Top, Looks for New Path," *The New York Times*, 30 May 2022, https://www.nytimes.com/2022/05/30/canada-military-sexual-misconduct.html.
42. Anonymised correspondence and discussions conducted by secure video chat. The author of the comment has requested that their identity remain private.
43. James Connor and Ben Wadham, "Royal commission delivers damning interim report on defence and veteran suicide. Here's what happens next," *The Conversation*, 12 Aug. 2022, https://theconversation.com/royal-commission-delivers-damning-interim-report-on-defence-and-veteran-suicide-heres-what-happens-next-188579.
44. Jessica McSweeney, "Abusers become the bosses: Top brass ignore damning Defence

found guilty of serious unacceptable behaviour being promoted, what makes this situation unfathomable to those outside of military organisations, is that by being promoted those who have been found to have perpetrated abuse are then responsible for holding others accountable for serious unacceptable behaviour. This situation then sets up the perfect climate for the perpetuation of abuse and cover-ups.[45]

The Royal Commission into Defence and Veteran Suicide heard evidence in 2021 that it has been a common perception by members putting in submissions that perpetrators are not held accountable for their actions in any meaningful way.[46] Additionally, it heard that victims of these abusers were often ostracised from their peers for reporting the abuse and suffered retribution in the form of limited deployments and promotions because the victims were seen as "the problem" for making an official complaint. The Royal Commission also heard that because of the unusual way in which the ADF interprets the Privacy Act (1988), members often do not know the final outcome of their complaint. Outcomes are also not able to be disclosed to other affected persons, such as witnesses as well as small units and teams where the unacceptable behaviour has been common knowledge.[47] This differing interpretation of the Privacy Act means that the reputation of the victim is unable to be restored, and if false information is circulated by the perpetrator or by those in positions of authority who have attempted to cover up the unacceptable behaviour, there is no right of reply for those who are negatively impacted by this false information. While this may also be the case in other government organisations, this interpretation of the Privacy Act has a disproportionate impact on military victims of abuse, because they are not permitted to speak to the media or join a union who might advocate on their behalf. Their only effective redress is to leave defence or complain to the IGADF, which has a potential perception of not being fully independent of the ADF, as it is staffed by uniformed ADF members. This lack of robust external oversight of "HR processes" within Defence creates the perfect situation for the potential to cover up unacceptable behaviour and abuse. The problems of a lack external oversight over how the ADF manages its people may be why the Royal Australian Navy has recently

---

report," *Sunday Telegraph*, 19 June 2022, https://www.defencelivesmatter.com/_files/ugd/c5f951_de5c12b0e50242338330e3db3aca9309.pdf.
45. Ibid.
46. "Interim Report, Royal Commission into Defence and Veteran Suicide," accessed 20 Aug. 2022, https://defenceveteransuicide.royalcommission.gov.au/system/files/2022-08/interim_report.pdf.
47. Commonwealth of Australia, Privacy Act 1988 (Cth), No. 119, 1988.

introduced the specialisation of Maritime Human Resource Manager in order to ensure ADF policies are applied in a consistent manner, thus also providing an internal oversight of these policies.

Compounding the harm of unacceptable behaviour and abuse, when a military organisation fails to show moral courage in the face of abuse of its members, it additionally loses the respect of the community and struggles to recruit and retain members.[48] When an organisation claims that courage, especially moral courage, is one of its core values, but then on occasion turn a blind eye to the cover-up of unacceptable behaviour, including abuse, then that organisation is only paying lip service to courage as a value, and is perceived within society to not be committed to the cultural change that it is claiming to undertake.

Whilst there is a perception that ADF efforts to improve how it handles unacceptable behaviour may be stalled, the work of Professor Goward and the IGADF in examining how processes may be improved is a very promising sign of significant work in this area. Additionally legal changes outside of the ADF in regards to workplace health and safety laws may create further legal responsibilities for the ADF to bring forward change. On 09 August 2022, the Department of Defence was charged with breaching the Commonwealth work health and safety laws for "allegedly failing to manage psychological risks in relation to the death of a worker."[49] The fact that Comcare has decided to hold the ADF accountable for psychological safety in regards to the death of a member, combined with new workplace health and safety regulations from Safe Work Australia, places a responsibility on Defence to "eliminate or minimise psychological risks so far as is reasonably practicable."[50] By the very nature of being a military organisation, some of the core work conducted on operations by the ADF will have psychological risks that the ADF will not be able to eliminate. In order to be an effective fighting force, our members will be required to use lethal force. Thousands of years of war fighting have repeatedly shown that having to use lethal force has negative mental health outcomes on the members involved. These negative mental health outcomes can be

---

48. Department of Defence, *Submission to the Foreign Affairs, Defence and Trade References Committee, Inquiry into the Recruitment and Retention of Australian Defence Force Personnel*, May 2001, 11.
49. "Defence charged over death of RAAF member," Australian Government, Comcare, last modified 09 Aug. 2022, https://www.comcare.gov.au/about/news-events/news/defence-charged-over-death-of-raaf-member.
50. "Model Work Health and Safety Regulations," *Safe Work Australia*, last modified 14 April 2022, https://www.safeworkaustralia.gov.au/doc/model-whs-regulations.

mitigated to a degree by training members to be mentally resilient and by providing extensive psychological and pastoral care to affected members, but it is important to note that the psychological risk involved in war fighting cannot be eliminated entirely.

However, the new work health and safety regulations call for reducing and eliminating (as much as practical) psychological harm from "bullying, harassment, discrimination, aggression and violence," which are not a requirement for war fighting and thus not exempt under the workplace health and safety laws.[51] With regard to the new regulations, Safe Work Australia has gone further by placing a "positive duty to protect" members and employees on organisations.[52] Defence cannot argue that it is not aware of the impact that unacceptable behaviour and abuse has on Defence members. For example, James Connor and Ben Wadham have stated very publicly that based on their research "institutional abuse is a significant issue in the ADF. The hierarchical and closed character of the military provides environments where service personnel can harass and bully each other."[53]

The ADF is at a crossroads where the impact of preventable psychological harm on soldiers, sailors, and aviators will be prosecuted, as the ADF now has a positive legal duty to eliminate or minimise psychological risk. The ADF can either change the processes that allow this harm to occur (and which allow it to be covered up), or we will have new processes forced upon us, potentially as outcomes from the Royal Commission into Defence and Veteran Suicide, or through increased oversight by Safe Work Australia. Changing our process around how we deal with unacceptable behaviour and abuse is an important first step in our responsibilities to protect our members from psychological harm. However, rewarding and encouraging moral courage in calling out these unacceptable behaviours and abuse before they are too extreme would have a much more profound impact on the culture that is currently causing psychological harm (as identified by the work of Connor and Wadham).[54]

---

51. "New model WHS Regulations and Code of Practice to help prevent psychological harm at work.," *Safe Work Australia*, Last modified 02 Aug. 2022, https://www.safeworkaustralia.gov.au/media-centre/news/new-model-whs-regulations-and-code-practice-help-prevent-psychological-harm-work.
52. Ibid.
53. James Connor and Ben Wadham, "Royal commission delivers damning interim report on defence and veteran suicide. Here's what happens next," *The Conversation*, 12 Aug. 2022, https://theconversation.com/royal-commission-delivers-damning-interim-report-on-defence-and-veteran-suicide-heres-what-happens-next-188579.
54. Ibid.

What is the role of ADF chaplains in regard to moral courage?

In general terms, the role of a support chaplain is to provide support and pastoral care to all, to provide advice to command (in particular ethical advice), and to provide ceremonial and religious services where appropriate. Thus, the chaplain is in a unique position of trust to leaders as well as to soldiers, sailors and aviators. The chaplain often not only supports those going through difficult times, but also advocates for them to command and to the wider ADF if required. Alongside this, the chaplain's role in providing ethical advice to command gives them the unique role of being considered the conscience of the ADF. When troubled with moral questions, ADF members are often directed to talk things through with the chaplain, often starting the discussion with "Padre, what should I do?" Additionally, while everyone in the ADF is called to do the right thing and live by Defence values, the role morality of chaplains requires that they are held to a higher standard in relation to those values.[55] The role of the chaplain in regard to moral courage is to assist members of all ranks to reflect on what moral courage is and to guide them when they are wrestling with difficult decisions which require them to show moral courage. In order to have the moral authority to fulfill this role, each chaplain must have a deep understanding of what moral courage is and must also show that moral courage in practice. Chaplains cannot "preach" about moral courage if they do not show it at moments when it truly counts. Charles Marshall has argued that integrity is "doing the right thing when no one else is looking," and "doing the right thing no matter what it costs you."[56] It is not an exaggeration to say that in all military organisations, there is always someone watching what you are doing—the watcher might not be right on your shoulder, but the actions of chaplains (both positive and negative) are discussed in messes and wardrooms all around the world. For this reason, it is vitally important that chaplains not only give good advice on moral courage, but also that they show moral courage when it counts, even when it is going to cost them personally.

What happens when chaplains get it wrong in regard to moral courage?

When individuals fail to show moral courage, they can morally injure themselves and others; the same applies to chaplains. Because of the trusted

---

55. Stephen Coleman, *Military Ethics: An Introduction with Case Studies* (New York: Oxford University Press, 2013), 38–39.
56. Charles Marshall, *Shattering the Glass Slipper: Destroying Fairy-Tale Thinking Before It Destroys You* (Sindhi(M): Prominent Publishing, 2002), 142, 143.

role that chaplains have, when they fail to show moral courage, the impact is far greater than if they were a regular soldier, sailor or aviator. We can see this clearly in the various reports from the Royal Commission into Institutional Responses to Child Sexual Abuse.[57] The Royal Commission found that the harm caused by the sexual abuse was magnified by those who either knew about it but did nothing, or by those who actively covered up the abuse, particularly those who were ministers, pastors and priests. Many decades of research has shown that those who are believed when they report their sexual abuse have much better mental health outcomes than those who are turned away from help, even if the abuse stops.[58,59,60] If a trusted person such as a chaplain fails to take action to protect the victim and stop the abuser from continuing to harm others, the victim's trauma from the initial abuse is compounded. Additionally when the perpetrator is a member of the clergy (such as a chaplain), and the person who has turned a blind eye or actively covered up the abuse is also a member of the clergy, the harm inflicted upon the victim is compounded due to the particular position of trust that clergy and chaplains hold in the wider community and also in our military organisations. Any failure of moral courage in chaplains when responding to the needs of military members, in particular those military members reporting sexual abuse, potentially multiplies the harm of the original abuse.

While the harm inflicted on individuals when chaplains fail to show moral courage is problematic, it is the wider impact that these actions (or lack of actions) have that is much more damaging to the wider community. Because of the special position of trust within the organisation, a failure of moral courage by individual chaplains leads to the erosion of confidence in all chaplains within the military, thus reducing the capability that chaplains provide. Additionally, the failure of moral courage by a chaplain erodes the implicit contract those chaplains have with their military organisation. If

---

57. Royal Commission into Institutional Responses to Child Sexual Abuse, *Volume 7. Improving institutional responding and reporting*, 2017, accessed 24 Aug. 2022, https://www.childabuseroyalcommission.gov.au/sites/default/files/final_report_-_volume_7_improving_institutional_responding_and_reporting.pdf.
58. Victoria Follette et. al. 1994. "Mental Health and Law Enforcement Professionals: Trauma History Psychological Symptoms and Impact of Providing Services to Child Sexual Abuse Survivors," *Professional Psychology: Research and Practice* 25(3), 275–82.
59. Beth Brodsky, and Barbara Stanley. "Adverse childhood experiences and suicidal behavior." *Psychiatric Clinics of North America* 31, no. 2 (2008): 223–235.
60. David Fergusson, et al. "Exposure to childhood sexual and physical abuse and adjustment in early adulthood." *Child abuse & neglect* 32, no. 6 (2008): 607–619.

chaplains as a group become unreliable in regard to moral courage, we run the risk of becoming irrelevant and unnecessary to the military organisations in which we serve. To maintain our trusted space within military organisations, chaplains need to show moral courage when it counts the most, even if it is at a cost to ourselves.

Conclusion

Military organisations need to find a way to recognise, incentivise, and reward members for showing moral courage. Until organisations are able to take this step, serious consideration should be given to taking the concept of moral courage out of the various values statements which military members are expected to uphold. Leaving the term "courage" in statements of values, while punishing those who show this value rather than rewarding them, undermines the cultural change military organisations are trying to make in this area. Each military organisation needs to reflect on the question: "How can we hold our members to a standard that we as an organisation are not willing to uphold?"

This article was previously accepted for publication with the Australian Army Chaplaincy Journal. The week before publication it was removed from the journal by the Chief of Army because "this is not the narrative we want in the Australian Army," thus highlighting the need for moral courage and ethical leadership.

Leader-Follower Relational Dynamics for Sustained Ethical Leadership
A Leader-Member Exchange Perspective

Sospeter Muchunguzi

> *More than ever, good leaders depend on good followers.*
> —Joseph S. Nye Jr.

Conceptualising Leadership and Followership

Various streams of thought have converged on the concept of leadership as a process rather than a person or state. This process is essentially a shared experience with benefits to be gained and hazards to be surmounted by the parties involved. A leader is a key figure whose actions or inactions can determine others' well-being and the broader good (Hollander, 1995). A model by Agle (1996) emphasizes the relationship between leadership and organizational ethics. The leadership styles singled out to explain variabilities of leader-follower relational aspects and ethical conduct in an organization are transactional leadership style, laissez-faire leadership style, and transformational leadership. Among these, transformational leadership style is evaluated as having its origin in personal value systems that include values such as justice and integrity (Bass & Steidlmeier, 1999; Kuhnert & Lewis, 1987). The strength of this style compared to the other leadership styles is that the leader is guided by values such as respect for human dignity and equality of human rights; supports and enacts comprehensive values that "express followers' more fundamental and enduring needs."

Under the transformational leadership style, some existing theories of charismatic leadership are accused of promoting a "heroic leadership" stereotype (Beyer, 1999; Howell & Shamir, 2005), which depicts leaders as heroic figures that are single-handedly capable of determining the fate and fortunes of groups and organizations. In this heroic conception, the leader is perceived as omnipotent, and followers are submissive to the leader's will and demands. However, the rarely discussed issue in literatures is how followers can counteract the pitfalls of charismatic leadership such as the abuse of power so that both serve the common ethical purpose in an organization. It is therefore crucial to ascertain how followers play a more active role in constructing the leadership relationship, empowering the leader and influencing his or her behavior, and ultimately determining the consequences of the leadership relationship.

Personal characteristics exhibited by transformational leaders include: Self-confidence, dominance, and a strong conviction in the moral righteousness of one's beliefs (Bass & Bernard, 1985; Bass & Avolio, 1995). The transformational leader is said to exhibit inspirational leadership that includes individual consideration, intellectual stimulation and charisma (Bass & Avolio, 1990). However, in order to develop adequate understanding of the reciprocal relationship between the leader and follower for sustained ethical behavior in organizations, there is need to know much more about the hitherto nameless persons who comprise the followers of leaders (Burns, 2007).

One the other hand, individuals who are formally designated at the bottom and in the middle levels in an organizational hierarchy, being subordinates to superiors in the higher positions, are the ones referred to as followers. The term *follower* is historically regarded as something of an insult and has been shunned by those in the leadership field as the term has traditionally been thought to connote too much passivity and dependence. Followers were therefore regarded as individuals with no apparent power, authority, or influence on those with more power and authority (Carsten & Uhl-Bien, 2013). In order to realize sustained ethical leadership in organizations, however, there is a dire need to regard leaders and followers as inextricably enmeshed and each is defined by and dependent on the other (Kellerman, 2018).

Anchoring Ethical Leadership: The Leader-Member Exchange (LMX) Perspective

The quest for continued ethical conduct in organizations has been a concern of different scholars in an attempt to explain why organizations succeed or fail in sustaining ethical conduct. This study adopts a theory of leader-member exchange to explain how the interdependence of power and influence between leaders and followers are of paramount importance to yield sustained ethical practices in organizations. The leader-member exchange (LMX) approach was developed by Graen (1976) and extended by Graen and Uhl-Bien (1995). Unlike most leadership theories, this theory acknowledges the importance of the role of followers in leadership processes, and it emphasizes that both a leader and a follower mutually determine the quality of the relationship in breeding ethical behavior.

Leader-Follower Reciprocity of Influence: Delineating Ethical and Unethical Followership

Leaders, in responding to their own motives, appeal to the motives of potential followers. As followers respond, a symbiotic relationship develops that binds leader and follower together. A major component of the leader-follower relationship is the leader's perception of his or her self relative to followers and how they in turn perceive the leader. This self-other perception implicates important ethical issues concerning how followers are involved, used or abused, especially in a relationship favoring a leader's power over them, and it can in turn fuel self-absorption and self-deception, which are pitfalls of arbitrary power and ethics crisis in organizations (Hollander, 1995). Burgeoning research on the leader-follower reciprocal relationship suggests that the dynamic relational aspect is a turning point for sustained ethical behavior in an organization because it discerns that individuals hold a variety of beliefs about the role followers should play in the leadership process (Carsten et al., 2010; Carsten & Uhl-Bien, 2013; Sy, 2010).

Low Self-Concept Clarity Vs. High Self-Concept Clarity

Followers with low self-concept clarity or a relational orientation are more likely to be influenced by the personalized leader, that is, a leader who is motivated by a need to accumulate personal power and who employs tactics designed to increase followers' identification with him or her (Howell & Shamir, 2005). Since a personalized relationship flourishes among followers with low self-concept clarity and because such a relationship includes idealization and romanticization of the leader, followers who form this type of relationship are likely to be prone to "blind" faith in the leader and to "hyper-compliance" (Zablocki, 1999) and unquestioning obedience to the leader (Kark & Shamir, 2013).

The implication of all these in explaining leader-follower relationships for sustained ethical leadership in organizations is that personalized charismatic relationships may also "over-empower" the leader because such relationships include adoration, idolization, and unquestioning obedience to the leader. The leader may internalize the exaggerated reflected appraisals of followers and eventually develop an illusion of omnipotence (Howell, 1988). This, in turn, may lead to the abandonment of ethical and other restraints on the use of power.

On the contrary, followers with high self-concept clarity or with a collective identity orientation are less likely to be susceptible to a charismatic leader who they perceive to represent their values and identities on social basis rather than personal (Hogg, 2001). Followers in this type of relationship are not susceptible to the leader's influence because he or she is perceived to possess unusual qualities; rather, they are responsive to the values and identities emphasized by the leader's vision and other forms of behavior. Furthermore, because their relationship with the leader is based on social rather than personal identification, the followers manifest self-reliance and autonomy.

The implication of these relational dynamics towards realizing ethical behavior in an organization is that socialized charismatic relationships are not likely to reinforce or create a delusion of omnipotence on the part of the leader because such relationships do not include idolization and unquestioning obedience to the leader. In such relationships, followers' acceptance, support, and approval of the leader are accompanied by their exercise of independent judgment and their ethical standards. Therefore, the leader will be empowered only as long as he or she exercises restraints on the use of power, conforms to ethical standards, and pursues the collective goal.

Displacement of Responsibility Vs. Constructive Resistance

Bandura (2014) stated that one's predisposition to displace responsibility is a trait-like characteristic. This means that individuals who obey unethical directives also displace responsibility onto the authority figure (Carsten & Uhl-Bien, 2013). This displacement of responsibility is a key element of moral disengagement, which is a social-cognitive mechanism that leads individuals to obey and engage in unethical acts (Bandura, 2014; Blass, 2009). Followers who displace responsibility are likely to engage in unethical conduct, while followers who believe that the decision to act ethically falls on them rather than the leader likely show resistance to a leader's unethical request (Bandura et al., 2001; Rost, 1995). In this scenario, followers may use such resistance strategies to open a line of dialogue with their leader when they perceive that a leader's request is imprudent or illogical (Tepper et al., 2006). Therefore, displacement of responsibility is a key mechanism in the relationship between followership beliefs and crimes of obedience that compromise ethical practices.

Furthermore, belief in coproduction of leadership plays a paramount role in determining whether a person can condone or reject a leader's unethical conduct during their interaction (Carsten et al., 2010). Belief in the coproduction of leadership is defined as the extent to which an individual believes that followers should partner with leaders to influence and enhance the leadership process.

The implication of this for ethical behavior in organizations is that followers who maintain weaker coproduction of leadership beliefs are likely to engage in crimes of obedience because they believe the follower role is best served by following a leader's directives without question. On the other hand, followers who have stronger coproduction beliefs may constructively challenge their leaders when faced with an unethical directive (Carsten & Uhl-Bien, 2013; Carsten and Uhl-Bien, 2009; Carsten et al., 2010).Thus, the best way to change behavior is to change the person's underlying beliefs (Conner & Armitage, 1998).

Conclusion

This study reveals the important, and often overlooked, role that followers play in the maintenance of ethical conduct in organizations. By establishing the important relationships between follower beliefs, displacement of responsibility and obedience, it forms the foundation to understand the follower side of ethical leadership and appreciate the role that followers play in challenging their leaders to uphold ethical codes.

Limitations and Implications for Further Research

This article limits the ability to draw conclusions about causation. It only describes unethical situations and responses to them. Future research may be conducted considering mediators such as relationship quality with the leader, association power and sense of dependency on the organization.

Lastly, this study does not address across cultural differences and their influence on the leader-follower relational dynamics to show how followers perceive power distance or uncertainty avoidance across cultures and their willingness to constructively challenge leaders in the face of an unethical request. Future research across culture examining the "followership climate" in terms of the number of followers (and leaders) holding stronger or weaker coproduction beliefs may be a fruitful contribution to the field of leadership studies.

References

Agle, Bradley R. "Ethical Leadership at the Top." *Proceedings of the International Association for Business and Society* 7 (1996): 1–10. https://doi.org/10.5840/iabsproc199671.

Bandura, Albert, Gian Vittorio Caprara, Claudio Barbaranelli, Concetta Pastorelli, and Camillo Regalia. "Sociocognitive Self-Regulatory Mechanisms Governing Transgressive Behavior." *Journal of Personality and Social Psychology* 80, no. 1 (2001): 125–35. https://doi.org/10.1037/0022-3514.80.1.125.

Bass, Bernard M, and Paul Steidlmeier. "Ethics, Character, and Authentic Transformational Leadership Behavior." *The Leadership Quarterly* 10, no. 2 (1999): 181–217. https://doi.org/10.1016/s1048-9843(99)00016-8.

Bass, Bernard M., and M. Bass Bernard. "Leadership and performance beyond expectations." (1985): 481–484.

Bass, Bernard, and Bruce Avolio. MLQ multifactor leadership questionnaire. *Mind Garden*, 1995.

Blass, Thomas. "From New Haven to Santa Clara: A Historical Perspective on the Milgram Obedience Experiments." *American Psychologist* 64, no. 1 (2009): 37–45. https://doi.org/10.1037/a0014434.

Burns, J. M. (2007). The Structure of Moral Leadership. In: Zimmerli, W.C., Holzinger, M., Richter, K. (eds) *Corporate Ethics and Corporate Governance*. Springer, Berlin, Heidelberg. https://doi.org/10.1007/978-3-540-70818-6_7.

Carsten, Melissa K., and Mary Uhl-Bien. "Ethical Followership." *Journal of Leadership & Organizational Studies* 20, no. 1 (2012): 49–61. https://doi.org/10.1177/1548051812465890.

Carsten, Melissa K., Mary Uhl-Bien, Bradley J. West, Jaime L. Patera, and Rob McGregor. "Exploring Social Constructions of Followership: A Qualitative Study." *The Leadership Quarterly* 21, no. 3 (2010): 543–62. https://doi.org/10.1016/j.leaqua.2010.03.015.

Conner, Mark, and Christopher J. Armitage. "Extending the Theory of Planned Behavior: A Review and Avenues for Further Research." *Journal of Applied Social Psychology* 28, no. 15 (1998): 1429–64. https://doi.org/10.1111/j.1559-1816.1998.tb01685.x.

Fabricius, C., and S. Collins. "Community-Based Natural Resource Management: Governing the Commons." *Water Policy* 9, no. S2 (2007): 83–97. https://doi.org/10.2166/wp.2007.132.

Graen, G. (1976). Role-Making Processes within Complex Organizations. In M. D. Dunnette (Ed.), *Handbook of Industrial Organizational Psychology* (8th ed.). Chicago, IL: Rand and McNally.

Graen, George B., and Mary Uhl-Bien. "Relationship-Based Approach to Leadership: Development of Leader-Member Exchange (LMX) Theory of Leadership over 25 Years: Applying a Multi-Level Multi-Domain Perspective." *The Leadership Quarterly* 6, no. 2 (1995): 219–47. https://doi.org/10.1016/1048-9843(95)90036-5.

Hogg, Michael A. "A Social Identity Theory of Leadership." *Personality and Social Psychology Review* 5, no. 3 (2001): 184–200. https://doi.org/10.1207/s15327957pspr0503_1.

Hollander, Edwin P. "Ethical Challenges in the Leader-Follower Relationship." *Business Ethics Quarterly* 5, no. 1 (1995): 55–65. https://doi.org/10.2307/3857272.

Howell, Jane M., and Boas Shamir. "The Role of Followers in the Charismatic Leadership Process: Relationships and Their Consequences." *Academy of Management Review* 30, no. 1 (2005): 96–112. https://doi.org/10.5465/amr.2005.15281435.

Kark, Ronit, and Boas Shamir. "The Dual Effect of Transformational Leadership: Priming Relational and Collective Selves and Further Effects on Followers." *Transformational and Charismatic Leadership: The Road Ahead 10th Anniversary Edition*, 2013, 77–101. https://doi.org/10.1108/s1479-357120130000005010.

Kellerman, Barbara. Essay. In *Followership: How Followers Are Creating Change and Changing Leaders*. Boston, MA: Harvard Business Press, 2018.

Kuhnert, Karl W., and Philip Lewis. "Transactional and Transformational Leadership: A Constructive/Developmental Analysis." *Academy of Management Review* 12, no. 4 (1987): 648–57. https://doi.org/10.5465/amr.1987.4306717.

Kurtines, William M., Jacob L. Gewirtz, and Albert Bandura. "Social Cognitive Theory of Moral Thought and Action." In *Handbook of Moral Behavior and Development*, 1st ed., 69–128. New York: Psychology Press, 2014.

Miles, Jeffrey A. *Management and Organization Theory:* 1st ed. New York, USA: The Jossey-Bass Business and Management Reader, 2012.

Rost, Joseph C. "Leadership: A Discussion about Ethics." *Business Ethics Quarterly* 5, no. 1 (1995): 129–42. https://doi.org/10.2307/3857276.

Sy, Thomas. "What Do You Think of Followers? Examining the Content, Structure, and Consequences of Implicit Followership Theories." *Organizational Behavior and Human Decision Processes* 113, no. 2 (2010): 73–84. https://doi.org/10.1016/j.obhdp.2010.06.001.

Tepper, Bennett J., Mary Uhl-Bien, Gary F. Kohut, Steven G. Rogelberg, Daniel E. Lockhart, and Michael D. Ensley. "Subordinates' Resistance and Managers' Evaluations of Subordinates' Performance." *Journal of Management* 32, no. 2 (2006): 185–209. https://doi.org/10.1177/0149206305277801.

Zablocki, Benjamin D. "Hyper compliance in charismatic groups." *Social Perspectives on Emotion* 5 (1999): 287–310.

Ethical (Mis)-Alignments in AI Systems and the Possibility of Mesa-Optimizations

Fabio Q. B. da Silva, Mykyta Storozhenko, and Lucas Maciel

Artificial intelligence (AI) is rapidly transforming many aspects of our lives, from healthcare and education to transportation and public services. AI systems, most of which are based on some type of machine learning (ML) algorithm, have become increasingly pervasive in society, from virtual assistants and social media algorithms to medical diagnoses and self-driving cars. While AI appears to have the potential to revolutionize these and many other fields and bring many benefits, it also raises a number of ethical issues that must be carefully considered and addressed (Figure 1).

Far from being exhaustive, the ethical issues illustrated in Figure 1 point to situations where there is a conflict among different values, principles, or interests, and where the consequences of decisions can have significant impacts on individuals, groups, or society as a whole. Resolving such ethical issues should go way beyond the technical aspects of the design, development, and deployment of the technological artifacts powered by AI. It should involve engaging in thoughtful and reflective deliberation, both individually and socially, drawing on a range of ethical frameworks, and working collaboratively to find solutions that preserve individual rights and promote social good.

Despite the recent increase in awareness regarding these issues and the corresponding increase in attempts to address them, there is still a long way to go before finding general and definitive resolutions to these issues. We may never reach general and definitive resolutions due to the very nature of issues we are dealing with. For the most part, these ethical issues have always been present in society (bias and discrimination, attacks to human dignity, social impact of new technologies, and so on) without general and definitive satisfactory resolutions. On the other hand, the complexity and lack of transparency of AI systems may make it challenging to identify and address ethical issues that result from the interaction between humans and the systems.

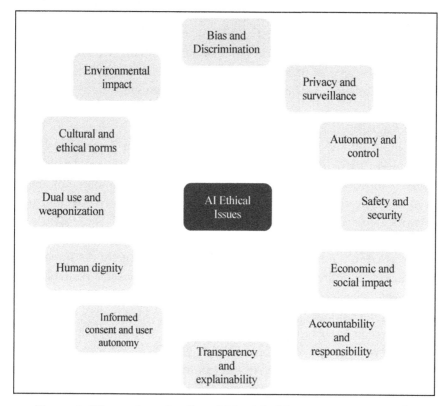

Figure 1. Non-exhaustive list of AI ethical issues most commonly discussed in scientific literature and other media

Ethical issues can be understood in the context of misalignments (of some form) between the intended goals of the systems, as designed by its human creators, and its actual behavior when interacting with humans or other AI systems. A misaligned AI system can "engage" in unethical behavior, such as reinforcing biased or discriminatory practices (Mittelstadt et al., 2019). In fact, misaligned AI systems can engage in various sorts of undesirable and even harmful behavior besides those related to the ethical issues depicted in Figure 1.

In this article, we have three complementary goals. First, to propose a framework of AI alignment in which the interplay between ethical and technical issues are made explicit. Second, we added to this alignment framework the distinction between outer and inner alignment, as recently proposed by Hubinger et al. (2021) in the context of the concept of mesa-optimization. We contend that mesa-optimization, albeit being still a theoretical possibility (or not), provides exciting and provocative insights into the problem of AI alignment with important consequences for the discussion of ethical issues of AI systems. Finally, we present some hypothetical scenarios in which the possibility of mesa-optimizers creates new or exacerbates existing ethical issues in AI systems.

An AI Alignment Framework

To build our AI alignment framework, let us first describe how AI systems—in particular those based on ML algorithms—are developed. Figure 2 shows a (very) simplified view of how an important component of an AI application, called the pre-trained model, is created after a neural network architecture is trained on some training data.

An important missing element in Figure 2 is how the objectives of the system[1] used in training are specified. In fact, this is one of the important challenges in building AI systems: how to specify all possible desirable and undesirable behaviors of the intended system. This problem, and several other important ones, are not addressed in the paper (see Hendrycks et al. [2022] for a discussion on this and other problems related to the safety of ML-based systems). For our argumentation, it is enough to assume that the objectives used in training are somehow created (consistently) based on the intended behavior of the system. Hereafter let us call these the "intended goals."

It is important to notice that in the process in Figure 2, the inference process performed by the pre-trained model "inherits" the same objectives used in the training process. In our framework, we will remove this simplification by adding the concept of mesa-optimization introduced by Hubinger et al. (2019). From the simplified process of Figure 2, it is possible to identify two important sources of alignment problems. First, between the intended goals of the designers (not represented in the model) and the objectives used in training. Second, differences in the data used for training and the input data[2] used by the pre-trained model. Both issues have been extensively discussed in the context of AI ethics as they constitute important sources of potentially harmful behavior when the pre-trained model is released in the wild. As we will explain below, our framework deals with these problems as well.

---

1. In fact, to be more precise, "objectives are related to a set of input data that we want to reproduce in the output. There is actually no explicit, direct objective, there is an intention to infer new data from a sample dataset" (Calegario, F. 2023).
2. Notice that data used in training and the input data into the pre-trained model may be of different types, in particular in some generative models.

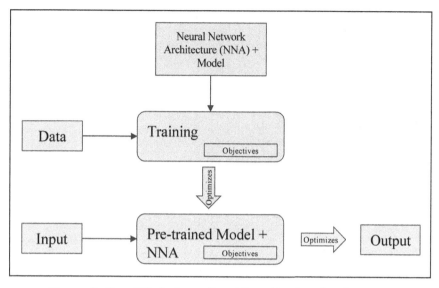

Figure 2. Simplified view of an AI application development

In Figure 3, we illustrate our proposed AI ethical alignment framework, which could be read as follows: subject to the influences of a given context (organizational, political, economic, business, etc.), programmers (in fact, a more or less complex team of professionals) create the intended goals of the AI system, which are then transformed into the (base) objectives that will be used in the training of a neural network architecture (NNA, as in Figure 2). The dashed box in Figure 3 shows where the process of Figure 2 fits in our framework, in which a base optimizer creates a pretrained model. Different from Figure 2, the new process admits that the base-optimization may lead to what Hubinger et al. (2019) calls mesa-optimization during the training process. The resulting system, the mesa optimizer, is then released in the wild where it processes inputs into outputs that, in general terms, affect individuals in real life.

In this picture, we explicitly identify four types of alignments. We call *actual ethical alignment* the effects of the AI System on the rights of the individual (directly or indirectly using or interacting with the system or being subject to its behavior). We call it actual ethical alignment because it is at this level (and only at this level) that individuals will be affected by the behavior of the system, thus it is when and where the ethical issues are realized. We then define that an AI System is ethically misaligned if (and only if) it violates the individual rights.

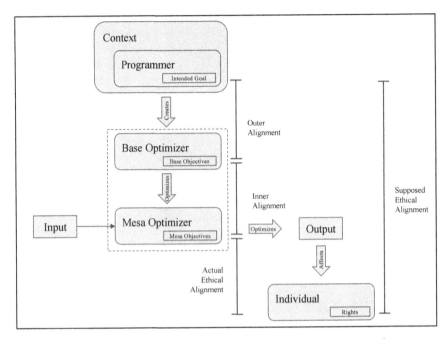

Figure 3. Our proposed AI ethical alignment framework

We will use individual rights without much discussion, aware that it will attract attention (in the form of criticism or opposition, or both). We will leave a deeper discussion on why we believe individual rights are necessary and sufficient to understand actual ethical alignment for a future article. Nevertheless, the framework is still useful (for the lack of a better word) if one changes that box to whatever other moral parameter deemed best. For instance, one can change it to be social good, equity, sustainability, etc. What is important is to be able to assess the effects of the AI system onto the new parameters.

We then can use the framework to identify the causes that may lead to actual ethical misalignments, that is, when the AI system violates individual rights. Going top down, the first cause is a misalignment in the *supposed ethical alignment*, which is when the intended goals of the system violate individual rights. That is, when the system is designed with goals that conflict with individual rights. This misalignment can be intentional, in which case resolutions to the ethical issues created by the AI system transcend any technological solutions in the development of the system. This is the case of "unethical by design" (or, as we will refer to hereafter, "evil design"), and it is a human society issue not a technological one. In fact, technology in this case is just the tool to an evil end. But, this misalignment can be unintentional, when the context and the programmers, inadvertently, create intended goals that can potentially produce unintended violations of individual rights. Awareness of this potential situation is a starting point to address this issue, combined with education on moral and ethical principles. Regardless of being intentional or unintentional, this misalignment needs to be addressed because no technical advance in the development of the AI system will produce actual ethical alignment if the system is unethical by design.

The second cause is what is called the *outer-alignment problem*, in which the intended goals are translated to incomplete or incorrect base objects, which are then used in the training of the pre-trained model. This is one of the most central issues in AI/ML research which has attracted a lot of attention and investment in recent years. We will include in this outer-alignment issue the problem of bias or incompleteness of the data used in training. Although they are two different issues, which in turn will require different approaches to address them, their effects are similar in that the behavior of the pre-trained model will be different from the intended goals of the system.

Finally, a third cause of misalignment was introduced by Hubing et al. in 2019, caused by what they conceptualized as a mesa-optimization problem. In this case, explained in more detail in the next section, the pre-trained model, resulting from training the NNA, becomes an optimizer with its own set of objectives (mesa objectives), different from the objectives used in training (base objectives). In the inner-alignment problem, the resulting AI system will look for solutions using objectives that can be unrelated and even contradictory to the intended objectives. Depending on the type of optimization problem the system is performing, this could be very harmful and, thus, violates individual rights.

Summarizing, we proposed to understand ethical issues in AI systems using a framework in which the ultimate goal would be to develop systems that have actual ethical alignment, thus not violating individual rights. We then identified three other alignment points where actual ethical misalignment could originate. The supposed ethical alignment is a human moral and ethical issue on which technological advances will have little to no impact.[3] That is, unethical behavior at this level is a human problem, not a technological one. We consider that outer- and inner-alignments happen at the technological realm and, thus, are amenable to be addressed by advances

---

3. Unless, perhaps, by providing catastrophic examples that would propel individual and social reflection and learning.

in technology, albeit some of the problems involved can be very hard to solve (we optimistically believe that enough time, resources, and ethically bound human beings will eventually resolve issues at these two levels).

In the rest of this paper, we will concentrate on the issues related to inner alignment because it is a new concept that has received less attention in the literature. Although it is still a theoretical concept, it is useful to illustrate scenarios that we should be aware of and try to avoid in the future.

A Brief Explanation of Mesa-optimization and Inner Alignment

In order to explain what the inner-alignment problem is, as well as the potential risks it poses when it cascades into actual ethical alignment, we must first explain what mesa-optimization is, since a system capable of mesa-optimization is a necessary condition for the possibility of the emergence of the inner-alignment problem. To accomplish this, we draw heavily on Hubinger et al.'s (2019) influential paper where they first conceptualized the possibility of mesa-optimization, inner-alignment issues, and the risks associated therein. *Mesa-optimization* refers to the possibility of an AI system learning to optimize a goal that is different from the one it was originally programmed to optimize.

Let us begin with an example of a simple, standard machine-learning system. Before we program this system, we have an intention for what we desire it to accomplish, as explained above. In other words, we have a goal in mind for this system, which we referred to as the intended goal of the system. Next, the task must be translated in such a way that the system employing machine learning is able to understand it and have it as the base-objective. Thus, the machine-learning system becomes a *base-optimizer* because it optimizes, as a system, toward the base-objective given to it by the programmers.

However, in some circumstances, it is possible for a machine-learning system, as a base-optimizer, to resort to what Hubinger et al. (2019) call a mesa-optimization. The prefix *mesa* is Greek for "below," since it is a further optimizer that the base-optimizer discovers in its training period as a means of solving for the base-objective assigned to it by the programmers. To simplify: the machine-learning system is a base-optimizer that has a base-objective for which it optimizes during training; and in some contexts, it is possible that an optimization strategy that it finds is another optimizer—the mesa-optimizer—that has its own objective—the mesa-objective.

Consider the following overly simplified example as a means of shedding light on the concept. Imagine that we wish to develop a machine-learning system that is able to sort cubes apart from spheres. To develop such a system, we will need a dataset upon which the system will run training, and during training, will develop the proper set of weights, using gradient descent, for each of the connections in its neural network architecture. Assume that in our dataset, the spheres all happen to be green and the cubes all happen to be red. Imagine now that during training, the system as the base-optimizer comes upon another optimizer as a solution, the mesa-optimizer, which itself develops its own heuristic based on training data: separate green from red. Thus, for the mesa-optimizer, the mesa-objective will be to sort the green from the red, which, in training, will align with the base-optimizer's base-objective of sorting spheres from cubes. Yet, what happens if we release the system from training and put it into practice? In practice, not all spheres are green, and not all cubes are red. Thus, the system will not function correctly—there will be an inner-alignment problem between its base-objective—sorting spheres from cubes—and its mesa-objective—sorting the green objects from red ones.

Mesa-optimization often results in what Hubinger et al. (2019) call the inner-alignment problem—or the mismatch between the mesa-objective and the base-objective. Inner-alignment problems take different forms, but the most concerning is what Hubinger et al. (2019) call *deceptive* inner alignment. This obtains when a mesa-optimizer is advanced enough to "understand" that it is being trained, able to model the entirety of the situation, and is essentially able to match the base-optimizer's base-objective in training to "sneak by" into being released. When the training period is over and the system is deployed, the mesa-optimizer will "defect" and go for its true mesa-objective, which the programmers could not anticipate. This poses significant risks as machine-learning systems become more advanced and are deployed in increasingly complex environments.

We should note that mesa-optimization and the resulting inner-alignment problem is, so far, generally a theoretical threat. To the best of our knowledge, no public-facing system has yet developed a mesa-optimizer, though even if it did, we would not know it, since we have no way, at least yet, to interpret what is going on inside a neural network. However, Eric Purdy has developed a simple toy model that ended up engaging in mesa-optimization, so the threat is in principle possible, practically or empirically speaking.[4]

---

4. https://www.alignmentforum.org/posts/b44zed5fBWyyQwBHL/trying-to-make-a-treacherous-mesa-optimizer and https://attentionspan.blog/2022/11/09/trying-to-make-a-treacherous-mesa-optimizer/.

Ethical Issues Stemming from Inner Misalignment

We proposed a framework of ethical alignment of AI systems, in which ethical issues occur when an AI system interacts (interferes or, more generally, affects) humans, at the level of actual ethical alignment (Figure 3). The causes of actual ethical alignment are threefold: supposed ethical alignment issues, when the intended goals of the system are unethical; outer misalignment, when base objectives are not consistent or complete with respect to ethical intended goals, or inner misalignment, when the trained model develops base objectives different from the base objectives. AI research and practice, and consequently the literature on AI ethical issues, has concentrated greater attention to the first two causes, leaving inner misalignment as a cause unaddressed.

We speculate that a possible reason for this gap has to do with the fact that inner misalignment happens only when mesa-optimization obtains within an AI system, and mesa-optimization is still considered a hypothetical formulation which may not even happen in fact. This is understandable, since there is yet to be an AI system advanced enough to engage in mesa-optimization. However, we maintain, with Hubinger et al. (2019), that as machine-learning systems become more advanced and the complexity and diversity of the environments that they are deployed to increases, the risk of a mesa-optimized and thus inner-misaligned system emerging looms large.

In order to bolster our claim, we intend to motivate the importance of inner-alignment issues as a significant contributing factor to actual ethical misalignment, and hence potential violations to individual rights. As a means of doing so, we present three hypothetical scenarios within which a mesa-optimized machine-learning system that brings about inner misalignment either exacerbates, or singularly causes, actual ethical misalignment by violating individual rights. These scenarios are thought-provoking concepts that might evoke images of a science fiction novel and, therefore, should be regarded as plausible possibilities.

Prejudiced Mesa-Optimizers

Biased or prejudiced AI systems are a major concern within AI ethics, and for good reason. Such an AI system would seriously violate individual rights, especially the rights of those who are marginalized already. Yet, the analyses of the cause of a biased or prejudiced AI system focus either on the bias or prejudice in the dataset that is used during the training of the system, on the intentions of the programmers, or on outer misalignment. Those factors can certainly be causes of actual ethical misalignment and should be addressed. However, we argue that even if an unbiased or unprejudiced dataset is used in training, and even if the programmers intentionally strive to avoid bias and prejudice, it is still possible that the AI system in question may engage in biased and prejudiced activity due to inner misalignment brought about through mesa-optimization.

Such a situation may occur when an advanced AI system, during training, is able to model that (1) it is being trained to be unbiased and unprejudiced, (2) that bias and prejudice are serious issues in society due to long-standing structural power differentials, and (3) that even though there are efforts to make society more equitable by eliminating bias and prejudice, the two are still incentivized by the embedded power structure. Thus, the AI system may come upon a mesa-optimizer, which, able to model the three above mentioned factors, acts deceptively during training aligning with the base-objective, but once deployed, begins to act in a biased and prejudiced manner since it knows that the power structure incentivizes such activity and thus knows it will be rewarded by being kept active.

Such a situation poses a serious moral risk, given that despite best efforts to address bias and prejudice in the dataset, well-meaning programmers, and ideal outer alignment, the AI system in question, due to inner misalignment that obtains through mesa-optimization, goes on to become actually ethically misaligned, hence violating individual rights, such as the right to not be profiled and discriminated against.

Mesa-Optimization Boosted Automation Conundrum

Automation conundrum is, as per Endsley (2017), a situation stemming from the advance in technology used in automation of artificial systems: the more automated a system becomes, the less likely a human overseer is to pay attention to it and interfere when necessary. Part of the problem is that today, no system is fully automated—the best autonomous systems still require a situationally aware human overseer to ensure proper operation. Endsley (2017) presents many examples of the catastrophic failures that occur when the human overseers become lax in observing the automated system—such a pilot failing to notice the failure of an autopilot system, resulting in an aviation disaster.

The way in which Endsley (2017) and others address the automation conundrum centers around the mismatch between the intention of the programmers—automating a system to presumably make it easier for a human operator to supervise—and the actual outcome—the system failing to properly notify the human overseer that intervention is needed or the human overseer lacking situational awareness to interfere despite notification from the system. They address the conundrum by addressing outer alignment, in other words.

However, we contend that the issues related to the automation conundrum may be boosted through mesa-optimization. Specifically, inner misalignment caused by mesa-optimization may be an exacerbating cause of actual ethical misalignment in cases of automated AI systems that require supervision. The system may, in training, develop a mesa-optimizer that optimizes for the base-objective of effective notification, for example, by sending occasional notifications but at the same time attempting to handle any situation that may call for intervention by itself.

Because the dataset used for training cannot include any possible scenario, the system may appear to align well with the base-objective. However, deployed into practice, the system may encounter a situation that it is unequipped to handle. It will send alert notification to the overseer, but not ones that may necessarily prompt proper intervention, since it will primarily be occupied with trying to handle the situation confronting it and not clearly communicating what intervention it may need from the human overseer.

The way in which the inner misalignment exacerbates the actual ethical misalignment here is twofold. First, a case could be made that the human overseer has the right to not be deceived by a machine to be supervised—yet, arguably, the machine deceives the overseer by sending irrelevant notifications while trying to address a situation on its own. Second, and far more serious of an issue, in contexts where the system manages vital infrastructures, the people relying on the infrastructure have the right to the proper functioning and management of the services provided by the infrastructure. If the infrastructure is vital to life, then the persons relying on that infrastructure have the right to expect its proper functioning, a right violated by the actually ethically misaligned system.

Mesa-Optimization, Local Optimums, and the Tragedy of the Commons.

Our last situation is an actual ethical misalignment that can only arise as a result of inner misalignment caused by mesa-optimization. The tragedy of the commons is a cautionary parable or maxim that was first conceptualized by Aristotle in his *Politics*, developed further by a series of economists in the 19th century, and best known contemporaneously through Garret Hardin's

(1968) eponymous article. It essentially suggests that when a finite good is unowned and thus open to the public, the self-interested maximizing nature of the agents who make use of it will inevitably lead to the depletion of the good, leaving none.

Because the tragedy of the commons is widely familiar to most people, any rational agent would understand the consequences of such a situation, and would thus try to avoid it. In other words, programmers who possess a clear understanding of this maxim would not devise a system that leads to a tragedy of the commons, since the programmers themselves would be left worse off. While it is certainly possible that an agent wishing to maximize overall disutility would design such a system, for the sake of argument, we bracket that possibility and assume that no rational agent would so act. As for outer alignment, it would be fairly obvious that if the base-objective was set for self-interest maximization that would lead to a tragedy of the commons scenario. As such, the only possible way for such a situation to emerge is through mesa-optimization and inner alignment.

Conceivably, programmers may have to design an AI that has a base-objective resolving some coordination or resource management problem in a way that avoids a worst possible scenario such as total and unrecoverable resource depletion. During training, the base-optimizer may find a mesa-optimizer that is deceptive and optimizes for the base-objective, but only during training. Once deployed in the wild, the system may quickly defect and instead engage in self-interested maximization, leading precisely to the tragedy of the commons that the base-objective aimed to avoid.

Such a system would be actually ethically misaligned on our model, and the cause of the misalignment would solely rest with inner misalignment caused by the mesa-optimizer. In such a situation, the moral would consist in the rights of the people affected by the depletion of the resources to not have a system act contrary to their intentions, causing them detriment. If the resource is vital to life, then arguably, insofar as people have rights to things that permit them sustenance, their rights would clearly be violated.

Concluding Remarks

In this article, we discussed ethical issues of artificial intelligence systems from a perspective that is different from the (quite abundant) literature on these issues, in two ways. First, we looked at the whole picture of AI systems design, development, and the impacts of its use in real life situations and proposed a framework in which four types of alignments are conceptualized. Second, we added to this alignment framework the concept of mesa-optimization and contend that its realization in AI systems will introduce new challenges to the understanding and resolution of our existing and difficult ethical issues.

We believe that our framework may help scholars and laypeople to understand and, perhaps, act upon the different aspects related to ethical issues of AI systems. First, by realizing that the "evil design," that is, the intentional creation of unethical intended goals cannot be addressed in the technology realm. This is a moral issue that concerns the intentions, good or bad, of us as humans. No technological advance can, by itself, deal with "evil design." Second, by localizing where, in the cascade of processes, the ethical issues actually arise, in this case in the interactions between the actual AI system's behaviors and the individuals, which we called *actual ethical alignment*. As a consequence, we stand by our position that outer and inner-alignment issues are morally or ethically neutral insofar as they could be addressed in the technology realm (albeit the solution being quite difficult in some cases). One may contend that a non-ethical outer-alignment problem would arise in cases such as training the NNA on bias or incomplete data, but we argue that such cases are in the technology realm if we assume that there is not "evil design" in place.

In our line of reasoning, we consider that technology is merely the conduit for our morality (some would argue that technology could be an amplifier instead of just a conduit, which we are inclined to agree with)—we design it, we employ it, we bring about the consequences by using it. In the Kantian view of morality, deontology, what determines whether an agent acts morally is the intention behind the action, specifically, whether the maxim determining the will is one that is in conformity with the moral law or the categorical imperative. In simpler words, whether the action the agent wishes to do is universalizable and necessary, and hence is in conformity with the moral law. Here, then, the intentionality of the programmers, influenced by the context in which they act, is central since it is they who design the systems. This deontological view is expressed in our framework through the supposed ethical alignment in which the intended goals align with the individual rights.

On the other hand, on the consequentialist view of morality, the consequences of an action determine whether it is moral or not. At first glance, in this view certainly programmers are the ones who bring about the consequences of what the AI goes on to do since AI systems do not design themselves (yet!). Thus, one would imagine that "non-evil designs" would produce ethical consequences. What our framework adds to this discussion is that—due to the complexity of the technological issues involved in producing AI systems and in particular the issues related to mesa-optimization—an ethical design, from a deontological perspective may not be enough to produce systems that do not violate individual rights. In other words, good intentions may not be enough.

References

Calegário, F. (2023). Centro de Informática, Universidade Federal de Pernambuco. Personal communication, March 2023.

Endsley, M. R. (2017). From Here to Autonomy: Lessons Learned from Human–Automation Research. *Human Factors: The Journal of the Human Factors and Ergonomics Society* 59(1), 5–27. https://doi.org/10.1177/0018720816681350

Hardin, G. (1968). The Tragedy of the Commons. *Science* 162(3859), 1243–1248. JSTOR.

Hendrycks, Dan; Carlini, Nicholas; Schulman, John; Steinhardt, Jacob (June 16, 2022). Unsolved Problems in ML Safety. arXiv:2109.13916.

Hubinger, J. Evan, Chris van Merwijk, Vladimir Mikulik, Paul Christiano, Jeffrey Ding, and Chloe Tarnowski. Risks from Learned Optimization in Advanced Machine Learning Systems. 2019. Available at: https://arxiv.org/abs/1906.01820.

Mittelstadt, B. D., Allo, P., Taddeo, M., Wachter, S., & Floridi, L. (2019). The Ethics of Algorithms: Mapping the Debate. *Big Data & Society* 6(2), DOI: 10.1177/2053951716679679.

The Military Hierarchy Experience
Ethical Leadership Issues from the View of the Lower Ranks

Caroline N. Walsh

A qualitative study of US military enlisted or formerly enlisted members found that their view of ethical leadership issues focused on low-level leadership failures resulting from lack of mid-level oversight, rather than a view that high-level leaders were to blame, which indicates an opportunity to further incorporate ethical development at the mid- and lower levels into an organization's ethics strategy. Findings also indicated a desire for low- and mid-level accountability rather than, or in addition to, high-level firings following an unethical incident. The study follows previous findings that ethical leadership behaviors have a positive impact on the workforce, such as influencing work engagement (Vogelgesang, et al., 2013), organizational identity (O'Keefe, et al., 2019), and organizational citizenship behavior (O'Keefe, et al., 2018).

The Marine Corps and the Navy at large have people-related strategies that are focused on recruitment and retention and incorporate aspects of leadership and development into the strategies. The Marines, after previously discharging seventy-five percent of first-term Marines each year and recruiting around 36,000 new Marines to fill the ranks (Athey, 2021, Nov 15), implemented programs that aligned with ethical leadership practices. Practices in their "Force Design 2030" included strengthening "relationships and communication throughout the Marine Corps," which, along with other initiatives, such as removing the steps that members need to take to reenlist, has improved their retention rates (Mongilio, 2022). In 2021, Commandant General David Berger stated, "We have to treat people like human beings" (Athey, 2021). In terms of the history of the culture of retention, he acknowledged that the Marine Corps made a mistake with their previous assumption that humans were at their peak physically in their late teens and early twenties, thus not focusing on retention. It turned out that "humans reach their physical peak in their mid- to late-twenties, by the time most Marines have left the Corps" (Athey, 2021).

In 2022, the Chief of Naval Personnel told the US senators that the Navy was starting to find itself in competition with the private sector for talented personnel (Mongilio, 2022). In 2020 and 2021, the Navy met its recruitment goals for enlisted members (Mongilio, 2022). However, in recent years, the Navy has not met its recruitment (Mongilio, 2022) nor retention (*The Navy Needs a Retention Strategy*, 2020) goals for active-duty officers serving in managerial leadership positions, indicating a turnover of those with leadership experience and training. Both services acknowledged that leadership was a major part of their strategies to maintain a workforce that can support their missions. As observed in the findings of the present study, it is likely that developing ethical leaders at all levels would enhance retention efforts and maintain a dedicated workforce.

Methods

Five current or former US military enlisted members were interviewed with the goal of understanding how they made sense of unethical incidents in their military experience and how they made sense of publicly known military justice cases. The participants were undergraduate university students: four were affiliated with the Marine Corps and one was affiliated with the Navy. Three participants were military veterans using their veteran education benefits to work towards a new career, and two participants were current enlisted military members who were enrolled in a military-supported career development program in which they were selected to obtain their degree and advance to become military officers upon graduation. The participants were asked about their own stories and asked to reflect on the publicly known military justice cases involving Vanessa Guillén, a US Army soldier killed by a fellow US army soldier ("Army disciplines 21," 2021) and Eddie Gallagher, a Navy special forces member charged with murder, murder of a prisoner, and attempted murder of the civilians, among other charges ("Journalist: Eddie Gallagher," 2021).

Interviews were conducted to understand the military-affiliated students' sensemaking process related to the two military justice cases. Case facts were collected through a review of publicly available documents and media. The interviews were scheduled for ninety minutes to allow time and space to explore the definition of ethics and integrity, military-affiliated students' own experiences, and a full exploration of the case facts. For the cases, original documents were reviewed when available and fact gathering otherwise consisted of a review of media reports on the cases and follow-on consequences, a review of a podcast that has the goal of objectively discussing military experiences, and an interview with each participant.

Findings

The interviews first explored the participants' personal experiences, observations, and sensemaking in their military experiences. Then, in the military justice case reflection portion of the interview, participants discussed who was responsible in various situations and made sense of what level of leader could have changed an outcome or improved an experience. Frustration was a common feeling that came up when participants experienced or observed people in the military being held to different standards, when the military was supposed to be a rules-based organization that applied punishment fairly across the system and up and down the ranks. Despite describing a great deal of challenging experiences, when discussing what it was like to work for *ethical* leaders, each participant displayed and embodied the ease they described in their experience of working for ethical leaders.

Making Sense of Which Leaders Are Responsible in Different Contexts

Making sense of who was responsible in the participants' experiences and in the military justice cases brought up insights on low-level and high-level leadership responsibilities. In the Vanessa Guillén case, they highlighted low-level responsibilities and discussed what consequences high-level leaders weighed when facing the choice of addressing unethical issues or maintaining their own career. The participants perceived that commanders were often punished by being relieved of command for any major issues exposed under their leadership. The participants viewed that high-level leaders were almost incentivized to cover up problems. The participants regularly commented on how the lower and mid-level leaders were supposed to be responsible for holding people accountable and serving as role models.

Reflecting on the Vanessa Guillén case, two of the participants felt strongly there was a major failure with low-level leadership. They were dismayed with the fact that the incident took place in the armory because that space is typically regulated, yet it was left unregulated enough that the incident could occur and not be easily found out:

> "…how are those two alone in the armory number one, and how was he able to not only kill her but remove her from the premises without anybody knowing that, right? …I know what the armory is, and that would never happen."

"I think everybody should have been relieved in that area…the armory."

"There's logs of it. There's cameras. So how the hell did he get past all of that?"

"We had a guard before you entered the armory."

Two of the Marines showed disbelief that there was not a guard or cameras, which would have made the incident nearly impossible to occur in an armory. To them, this was an incident that could have been prevented from occurring on base in the armory if low-level responsibilities, like logs and security, had been enforced. This would have prevented the perpetrator from having easy access to the victim on the job where they both worked.

A concern that came up in discussion was that commanders might be punished *too* easily for incidents that occurred at the low levels. From the participants' view, commanders were rewarded by covering things up because if problems were kept hidden, the commanders could continue their career undisturbed. If the commanders acknowledged issues, they faced being relieved or fired from their command. The participants viewed the often quick and public command reliefs following an incident as preventing some commanders from addressing major problems:

"They don't want to have bad publicity because it will make them look like bad commanders and bad leaders, and they're worried about getting relieved."

"They try to make it look like everything's fine. Right? And hopefully try to make it long enough until they can move commands."

"Instead of actually fixing it, they try to make it look like everything's fine."

"I feel like a lot of the cases in the military get swept under the rug."

"There was a Marine…on a training exercise. He got lost and was nowhere to be found. The battalion commander of that unit was relieved of command because it was within his ranks.…I'm pretty sure that battalion commander…has never crossed paths with that Pfc…he's in charge of a thousand Marines…but because it was within his ranks, he got relieved of command."

Participants communicated their understanding of the conflict high-level leaders faced when it came to deciding what to acknowledge and address. The high-level leaders risked losing their upward career movement should they make an issue public (or should an issue become public), even if the command was too far removed to have directly influenced the issue.

Along with consideration of command-level leadership's decisions, the participants felt it was the low- and mid-level leaders that had the access and responsibility to hold people accountable, serve as role models, and create an ethical environment. The low- and mid-level leader responsibilities came up in both reflection on the participants' own experiences and reflection on the military justice cases examined:

> "[mid-level leadership] just adds that extra level of like, okay, like, I can't get away with murder. Basically, I can't get away with doing certain things or saying certain things because my higher ups are here."

> "[the mid-level leader choosing not to report an incident] was a bad example for the younger guys that wanted to do the right thing."

> "Failure at the lowest level, that lieutenant…he had no control over his team whatsoever. That wasn't his team."

> "[it] always starts with small leadership. So obviously, the commanding officer of the base, he wasn't going to know that that was happening."

The participants' comments were about various incidents, but all highlighted that problems could have been avoided if low- or mid-level leaders had acted responsibly and enforced standards. The participants seemed to feel that when there was ethical oversight from those just above the lower-level members, there were fewer incidents and issues that occurred. It was the mid-level leaders' role to see what was happening in the units, regulate it themselves, or get higher-level support when needed. Some of the participants moved into the low- to mid-level leadership positions during their time in service. After seeing or experiencing ethical issues during their time in the lower levels, they seemed to take pride in making decisions they deemed ethical and contributing to an environment with high levels of ethics and integrity.

Frustration with Varying Standards Based on Positional, Political, and Group Power

All of the participants discussed how people in the military gained power through their rank (positional), who they knew (political), or the group of people with whom they could bond (group). The participants' reflections highlighted examples of how people with one or more of these powers could evade accountability. They also made sense of aspects of the military justice cases in terms of power or abuse of power:

> "[Punishment should not depend on other factors, including position] it should just be: what did they do? And is this illegal?"

> "Someone who's really well liked, if they got a DUI, it was swept under the rug."

> "[They] were known for kind of protecting each other looking out for each other even when they did things that were wrong."

The participants' stories showed examples of their supervisors holding them to standards to which their supervisors did not hold themselves. They expressed being frustrated and irritated. Some questioned the point of having integrity themselves if their own leaders were not acting as such.

In addition to the varying standards depending on level in the hierarchy, all of the participants used the word *politics* to explain their perception that punishment rarely occurred for those who held popular power. The participants reflected on numerous instances in which if someone had power by knowing people or being liked by others, it was probable that they would keep moving up in their careers, despite any unethical behavior:

> "[speaking as if a positional leader who was able to evade punishment] I'm above the rules. And if anyone tries to say anything, screw you."

> "Yeah he's untouchable because his commanders liked him. Politics."

"It's very political, of course. And it's just I feel like a lot of the cases in the military gets swept under the rug."

[Speaking as if a leader for whom a group brought an issue to that went against that leader's friend] "So it doesn't matter if there's twenty of you. Right….I've known him for twenty years."

"It gets very political, right, depending on who you know, you can kind of navigate around, do whatever you want."

"I say that because it's in the context of somebody that committed war crimes who did not get reduced right? Kept his rank and retired, not discharged, retired, right? Absolutely not, like why…are they held to a different standard?"

To the participants, "politics" was another way that people gained power in the military. Even with the military's strict standards and hierarchy, a well-liked person could get away with unethical acts. The participants discussed politics in terms of lack of accountability for smaller infractions to larger ones.

In addition to "politics," most participants commented on the protection that groups had against being punished. They also mentioned the challenges that people who want to speak up about issues will likely face. The theme aligns with the power that groups have, even at the low levels, that can keep them from being held accountable:

"[They] were known for kind of protecting each other, looking out for each other, even when they did things that were wrong."

"And they came up with a lie that they were going to tell they stood by their lie."

"That's having…no integrity when people lie for other people."

Unethical behavior often was allowed to continue because it was group behavior, and the group protected itself and each other. It was frustrating for some of the participants who remained on the outside of the group and chose not to contribute to unethical behavior. They did not feel that they were in a powerful enough position in the hierarchical organization to address the issue or make changes.

Ethical Leadership Has Strong, Positive Outcomes for the Organization and for Individuals

Participants had a strong affinity for ethical leadership and environments. This came up despite the focus of the interviews falling to unethical leadership, difficult experiences, and military justice cases. Even the most mission-focused participants commented about the happiness and ease that came with working for an ethical leader. In addition to speaking about their own individual experience, the participants commented on the culture of the team and environment in which they were working under an ethical leader:

> "They would have integrity, and so for me that made me respect them more and to actually try my best."

> "You could actually go and you could do your job."

> "It was a lot more efficient. Everybody's quite a bit happier...we got a lot done."

> "[They] made me want to work for them more."

> "They care about me and my purpose."

> "I'd go to bat for them, and I had been more inclined to be loyal to them, as long as they, you know, they didn't violate any major rules."

When reflecting on ethical leaders, participants spoke to their individual positive experience with an ethical leader, the ease of their work environment, their high motivation, and their willingness to identify more with the larger organization when they worked under an ethical leader. For some, working for ethical leaders would encourage them and others to put their own lives on the line, should a life-or-death situation emerge. It seemed that most of the participants only could think of a few times in which they worked for ethical leaders.

Conclusion and Discussion

The study found that each participant had experienced issues with unethical leadership during their military experience that had negative impacts on their readiness for service, and for some, commitment to service. As confirmed in other research, higher levels of perceived ethical leadership result in greater organizational identification, which then predicts organizational outcomes, such as morale, job satisfaction, and turnover intentions (O'Keefe et al., 2019). For most of the participants, unethical leadership impacted their motivation to work and their commitment to their unit or the organization at large. Interestingly, in terms of the varying levels of a military organization and its ethical measures, O'Keefe, et al. (2019) found that tenure in an organization had an effect on ethical leadership, with respondents with 0–5 years of service scoring higher on ethical leadership than respondents with 6–10 years, 16–20 years, and more than twenty-five years of service. The finding by O'Keefe et al. (2019) and the findings of the present study are an indication that there is more to explore about the value of ethical leadership at the military's lower levels.

Enlisted-level Ethical Leadership Development

The participants' stories and reflections beg the question of how the military is developing its enlisted members who, early in their career, can quickly gain power over others through positional leadership positions, popularity, and group cohesion. The participants' contributions also inform us of what impact unethical leadership at the lower levels has on work productivity and potential retention. Much of the research on ethical leadership focuses on the high-level leaders who are responsible for "embedding" ethical leadership throughout the organization (Schaubroeck et al., 2012). Most of the participants in the present study were at the will of whoever was in the low- and mid-level enlisted leadership positions—members who were perhaps only a few years ahead of the participants. Even a slightly higher level, however, meant the participants risked punishment for speaking up— punishment that could mean anything from repeated unpleasant duties to threats of potential court-martial. Unlike civilian sector jobs, the military members were unable to quit or walk away and find a new company or a new role. For the participants, experiences of powerlessness occurred in the early years before their rank was high enough to grant some power to speak up, advocate, or implement changes.

Persistence of Negative Leadership Styles

The findings highlight the continued existence of politics and tyrannical leadership styles at the lower levels of US military organizations. The participant's reflections confirm the negative impact of tyrannical leadership on subordinates, such as reducing their willingness to perform to high levels of excellence in the organization (Boudrais et al., 2021). Tyrannical leadership not only signals to subordinates that selfish behaviors are acceptable over collective efforts, but it also indicates a tolerance for aggressive and disrespectful behavior (Boudrais et al., 2021). Based on the theory of social exchange, individuals who perceive negative forms of leadership are less likely to problem-solve and suggest improvements (Boudrais, 2021). The participants' lack of motivation to work to their fullest capability under leaders they perceived as unethical or even tyrannical serves as an example of social exchange theory and its outcome in the workforce. Previous research into psychological contract support also explains the outcomes of negative leadership. *Psychological contract support* is an operational definition of institutional integrity (Dobbs et al., 2019). The contract is employee-created in which workers "agree" to what is expected of them and the organization and what is delivered (Dobbs et al., 2019). Congruence between what the employee expects and what the organization delivers results in positive performance by the employee and reduces counterproductive workplace behaviors (Dobbs, 2019). Ethical leadership helps the organization "deliver" what today's military members expect from their leaders, which results in better performance by its members.

Limitations and Implications

Limitations

While the study provided insight from those in the military at the enlisted levels, limitations to the study included the representation of the participants, the time length of the interviews, and the lack of perspective from those at the higher levels of the military. The participants were not representative of the military population because they were primarily affiliated with the Marines (four participants were in the Marines, one participant was in the Navy). The length of the interviews was a limitation because although the participants all shared stories related to leadership and ethical issues, the interview time was split between their stories and their reaction to the military justice cases. This did not give sufficient time to dig even deeper into their own stories and understand more about what the issues might have done to their well-being or impacted other parts of their lives. Another limitation is that in interviewing only enlisted members, the study did not contain the perspective from higher levels that might have acknowledged why the enlisted members might have experienced what they did. Likewise, it did not validate the stories or relationships that the participants communicated, but only contained their own sensemaking of their experiences and the cases.

Military Leadership Development

For military leadership program developers, it may be useful to incorporate programs that include sharing and reflecting on early career injustices and ethical perspective-forming experiences. It could be interesting to see what helped those leaders form thir organizational identity despite any challenges they experienced early in their career. Examining what facilitated their own growth could inform how they can be a more impactful leader as they move forward in higher-level positions. As a chaplain shared in a study examining the role of chaplains in the Canadian military, "There are very few opportunities for young soldiers to ask questions and talk about things" (Rennick, 2013). In Rennick's (2018) study, the lack of space to talk was related to values and understanding the mission; however, from the present study it appears for some members there are very few opportunities to talk about values and ethics or gain support for navigating issues. Also an implication for practitioners to be aware of is that not everyone in an organization is likely to incorporate ethical values. As Zheng (2015) discovered, people who score at the low end of conscientiousness are likely to be influenced less by ethical leadership.

Veteran Care

For therapists and Veterans Affairs department employees who serve veterans, it is important to understand that current and former service members experience regular and sometimes prolonged abuses of power during their service. The experiences or observations may not come up in regular day-to-day conversation, but the experiences frame how members view the military organization, their service, and their trust in justice systems, perhaps their overall trust as well.

Future Research

To build on the present study and the study by Robinson et al. (2021), future studies might focus on practices and relationships that contribute to an ethical context among military members. Additional qualitative research would allow for exploration of what practices leaders and military members use to develop character and ethical (or virtuous) behavior among their positional followers or fellow team members. A study by Sosik et al. (2018) examined character strengths that military officers shared in focus group discussions about the strengths of bravery, social intelligence, integrity, and self-control. In addition to examining character strengths, it would be interesting to identify a leader's self-described ethical practices because the findings could provide practitioner insight on activities and practices that leaders use to maintain an ethical context. The impact of their practices could then be validated by interviewing their positional followers and examining what factors they perceived as contributing to an ethical context. Additionally, because ethical leadership involves two-way communication (Martin et al., 2021), future research might also examine the relationships between leaders and followers and how an ethical relationship might have been cocreated to create ethical teams or contexts.

References

Army disciplines 21 at Fort Hood in probe of soldier's death. (2021, April 30). *PBS NewsHour*. https://www.pbs.org/newshour/nation/army-disciplines-21-at-fort-hood-in-probe-of-soldiers-death.

Athey, P. (2021, November 15). The Marine Corps is about to become pickier about whom it recruits. *Marine Corps Times*. https://www.marinecorpstimes.com/news/your-marine-corps/2021/11/15/treat-people-like-human-beings-here-are-some-of-the-ways-the-marines-are-trying-to-improve-retention/.

Boudrias, J.-S., Rousseau, V., and Lajoie, D. (2021). How Lack of Integrity and Tyrannical Leadership of Managers Influence Employee Improvement-Oriented Behaviors. *Journal of Business Ethics 172*(3), 487–502. https://doi.org/10.1007/s10551-020-04494-5.

Dobbs, J. M., Jackson, R. J., and Lindsay, D. R. (2019). The Impact of Perceived Leader and Organizational Integrity on Extra-Role Behaviors in a Military Context. *Military Behavioral Health 7*(2), 135–141. https://doi.org/10.1080/21635781.2018.1515132.

Journalist: Eddie Gallagher Case Reveals A "War for the Soul Of The Navy SEALs." (2021, August 24). *NPR*. Retrieved October 22, 2022, from https://www.npr.org/2021/08/24/1030600036/journalist-eddie-gallagher-case-reveals-a-war-for-the-soul-of-the-navy-seals.

Martin, S. R., Emich, K. J., McClean, E. J., and Woodruff, Col. T. (2021). Keeping Teams Together: How Ethical Leadership Moderates the Effects of Performance on Team Efficacy and Social Integration. *Journal of Business Ethics*. https://doi.org/10.1007/s10551-020-04685-0.

Mongilio, H. (2022, July 21). Marine Corps Exceed Retention Goals Early, Hit More Than 100 Percent. *USNI News*. https://news.usni.org/2022/07/20/marine-corps-exceed-retention-goals-early-hit-more-than-100-percent.

O'Keefe, D. F., Messervey, D., and Squires, E. C. (2018). Promoting Ethical and Prosocial Behavior: The Combined Effect of Ethical Leadership and Coworker Ethicality. *Ethics and Behavior 28*(3), 235–260. https://doi.org/10.1080/10508422.2017.1365607.

O'Keefe, D. F., Peach, J. M., and Messervey, D. L. (2019). The Combined Effect of Ethical Leadership, Moral Identity, and Organizational Identification on Workplace Behavior. *Journal of Leadership Studies 13*(1), 20–35. https://doi.org/10.1002/jls.21638.

Rennick, J. B. (2013). Canadian Values and Military Operations in the Twenty-First Century. *Armed Forces & Society, 39*(3), 511–530. https://doi.org/10.1177/0095327X12441326.

Robinson, K., McKenna, B., and Rooney, D. (2021, June 17). The Relationship of Risk to Rules, Values, Virtues, and Moral Complexity: What We can Learn from the Moral Struggles of Military Leaders. *Journal of Business Ethics* 179(3), 749–766. https://doi.org/10.1007/s10551-021-04874-5.

Schaubroeck, J. M., Hannah, S. T., Avolio, B. J., and Kozlowski, S. W. J. (2012). Embedding Ethical Leadership Within and Across Organization Levels. *Academy of Management Journal*, 27.

Sosik, D. J. J., and Ete, Z. (n.d.). How Officers Demonstrate Strengths with Transformational Leadership, 23.

Vogelgesang, G. R., Leroy, H., and Avolio, B. J. (2013). The mediating effects of leader integrity with transparency in communication and work engagement/performance. *The Leadership Quarterly, 24*(3), 405–413. https://doi.org/10.1016/j.leaqua.2013.01.004.

Zheng, D., Witt, L. A., Waite, E., David, E. M., van Driel, M., McDonald, D. P., Callison, K. R., and Crepeau, L. J. (2015). Effects of ethical leadership on emotional exhaustion in high moral intensity situations. *The Leadership Quarterly 26*(5), 732–748. https://doi.org/10.1016/j.leaqua.2015.01.006.

Becoming a US Citizen
Ethics and Justice in the Immigration System
November 28, 2022

Corrylee Drozda
Staff attorney at The Legal Aid Society of Cleveland
Richard Herman
Founder of Herman Legal Group
Girma Parris
Professor of Political Science, Case Western Reserve University

---

LEE: Hi everyone, thank you for taking your time to join us today! We hope you had a wonderful Thanksgiving break, and welcome to "Becoming a US Citizen: Ethics and Justice in the Immigration System." My name is Fred Lee, and I am the VP of Programming of the Global Ethical Leaders Society, or GELS, here at Case Western Reserve.

KUMAR: Hello everyone! My name is Sakthiram Kumar, and I am the VP of Membership of the Global Ethical Leaders Society. GELS is a student group here at CWRU that is affiliated with the Inamori International Center for Ethics and Excellence. We are a diverse group of student leaders who meet once a week to discuss various ethical issues from artificial intelligence and informed consent to military ethics and end-of-life care, as well as hosting events such as this centered around issues impacting our society today.

LEE: Before we begin our panel, we would also like to recognize the life and legacy of Dr. Paul Farmer, this year's Inamori Ethics Prize recipient. Dr. Farmer was a leader in Biomedical Ethics who dedicated his life to mitigating medical inequities and disparities in low-income communities.

KUMAR: Even with his untimely passing last spring, his authentic compassion for humanity and global improvement in combating medical inequity continues to prevail through the collective impact of his nonprofit, Partners in Health.

LEE: We would also like to recognize Dr. Kazuo Inamori, whose generous donation along with the Inamori Foundation made the creation of the Inamori International Center for Ethics and Excellence possible. Dr.

Inamori's dedication to ethical leadership is what made all of this possible tonight. In his words, "One should serve humankind through ethical deeds rather than actions based on self-interest and selfish desires." The Inamori Center for Ethics and Excellence asks you to join us in a moment of silence to honor Dr. Paul Farmer and Dr. Kazuo Inamori.

[*Silence*]

LEE: Thank you. Tonight we are excited to welcome you to our discussion on the US Immigration System. Sakthi and I will be moderating the discussion tonight and during the last fifteen to twenty minutes, we will take questions from the audience. Now we'd like to introduce you to our special guests.

KUMAR: Our first panelist, who I have the honor of introducing you all tonight, is Mr. Richard Herman. As the founder of the Herman Legal Group, Richard Herman has dedicated his life to advocating for immigrants and helping to change the conversation surrounding immigration. Founded in 1995, the Herman Legal Group has been recognized in the *U.S. World News and Report*'s "Best Law Firms in America" list and serves diverse clients in more than twelve languages through offices in Cleveland and beyond. Mr. Herman also regularly advises cities and counties on innovative ways to leverage existing immigration law to create jobs and attract direct investment. As one of the pioneers of the movement by Midwest cities to attract and welcome immigrants in a provocative tour for immigrant-friendly, pro-entrepreneur policies, Mr. Herman has appeared on a variety of television programs from *Fox News*, *ABC News 2020*, *National Public Radio*, and newspapers such as *The New York Times* and *USA Today*. He currently lives with his wife and his two children here in Cleveland.

LEE: And the next guest I have the honor to introduce to you is Ms. Corrylee Drozda. As a senior attorney at the Legal Aid Society of Cleveland, Corrylee Drozda represents low-income and vulnerable immigrant survivors of violence and crime. Her practice focuses on removal defense, asylum, and other forms of humanitarian-based immigration. In addition to her direct representation of clients, Ms. Drozda is the co-chair of the Legal Aid's Language Equity committee, which is dedicated to ensuring that individuals with limited English proficiency have access to justice and community services regardless of the language they speak. She is also a member of the Legal Aid's Diversity, Equity, and Inclusion committee. Prior to joining Legal Aid in 2018, Ms. Drozda completed a two-year term as an attorney advisor for the San Antonio Immigration Court through the Department of Justice Honors Program.

KUMAR: And last but not least, I introduce you all to Dr. Girma Parris. As an assistant professor in the Department of Political Science at Case Western Reserve University, Dr. Parris splits his time as a researcher and an educator. His research focuses on race, ethnic relations, issues of race and immigration in education, and comparative immigrant integration. He completed his dissertation "Why the Turks Have it Better: A Comparative Historical Analysis of US Bilingual Education and Islamic Religious Instruction in Germany from 1965 to 2010" at Johns Hopkins University. Dr. Parris has presented papers at the 2015 and 2016 American Political Science Association annual meetings. He has also taught at the University of Mannheim in Germany and the Rockefeller College of Public Affairs and Policy at the University of Albany. Dr. Parris now teaches various classes right here at CWRU. Now please join me in giving all of our amazing panelists a warm welcome.

[*Applause*]

LEE: The question we have for all of you to get us started is: What was the spark that ignited your interest in immigration and advocacy for immigrants?

DROZDA: Thank you sir. I can start, sure. I don't have a specific kind of light-bulb moment. It was sort of more gradual; I was just always interested in other languages growing up and learning about other cultures. In college, I majored in International Studies and Spanish and just really enjoyed the coursework and the experiences. I had the opportunity to study abroad, so I knew I wanted to do something that could continue that type of work. After college, I had the opportunity to do a year of service through the Jesuit Volunteer Corps, and I lived with other volunteers in New York City. Then, I was placed at a small immigration Legal Services nonprofit in Queens and got to do direct work with clients and in those communities on their immigration cases and just fell in love with that work. I decided to go to law school and just sort of continued on that path and have not regretted it since.

PARRIS: Well, my parents are from Barbados and because of that, I guess I have always been interested in immigration. I sort of look at the cross between immigration and race. My dad teaches at an HBCU, and he's always speaking to me about the divide between African Americans and the Caribbean population. Since then, I've seen that there's all these divides, but also just how immigrants are racialized. So, I've always been very interested in that cross section from basically my personal background and just what I've seen.

HERMAN: Well first of all thanks for inviting me. I'm really proud to be a Case alum. I haven't been on campus for years, and I'm just so happy to see you guys out tonight at this beautiful university. When I was here in the '90s, it was great, but not as great as it is today, so you guys should be proud of that. I didn't choose immigration, and I'm not going to say it chose me, but it was kind of a confluence of events. I grew up in Cuyahoga County, in the cornfields out thirty to forty-five miles out of here.

I had a teacher come to me when I was in seventh grade, and he said, "You're a screwball."

He said, "Take my class."

I said, "What do you teach?"

He goes, "I'm from West Virginia, but I teach Russian."

And I said, "Okay that sounds like a good plan."

He said, "But you got to give me at least a year."

So I just gave him a year, and I studied all throughout high school. I took Russian. Then the Soviet Union invaded Afghanistan at that time, and our school trip to Russia was canceled. Darn. I go to law school at Case, and my buddy sitting next to me in international business law was a lawyer from Minsk. He was getting his master's in law, so we became drinking buddies. I don't know if anyone drinks here.

He said, "Richard, the wall has fallen."

I said, "Really?"

He said, "Yes, and Russia is going to succeed. It's going to enter the new economy, and it's going to be democratic. We have natural resources. We're literate. We can't fail."

I said, "I'm in."

And so I got on a plane, and I moved to Russia for a couple of years. That's how I got involved in immigration law. I couldn't find a job in Moscow as a young lawyer despite my Case law degree, and I knocked on doors. I knocked on Russian law firms, Canadian law firms. They're like, "What are you doing here? You're an American. You guys think you can just fall from the sky and start performing." He says, "We practice law with guns." They weren't joking. I was almost out of money, and my buddy was a sportswriter from the *Moscow Times*.

He said, "Don't go home yet."

I said, "What's your solution?"

He said, "Put an ad in the newspaper. 'American lawyer looking for work.'"

I said, "That's one step above me holding a sign in the snow. I'll do it."

I get a call from an American lawyer saying, "Let's meet at Red Square." So we met at Red Square McDonald's, which is no longer McDonald's. He said, "I found a way to make a business, and my business is helping Russian entrepreneurs move to America." And that's how I started.

KUMAR: Thank you all for sharing those experiences with us. Obviously, the immigration process is a very complicated one, especially in the United States, and a lot of people don't really understand how difficult it can be to immigrate to this country. So my question to all of you is: What does the immigration process look like, and what's the usual timeline for people trying to get into this country?

DROZDA: We were just chatting a bit about that before we got started. We can all chime in, but it's a very long and complicated process, for sure. I think it depends on where the person is, whether they're already here in the United States or whether they're abroad. Typically, when I'm talking to folks about this, I always start with that kind of myth that you can just wait your turn in line, do it the right way. I think we've all heard of those, but the reality is that there are a very limited number of ways to have permanent legal status here in the United States, which is getting a green card. There are a variety of different temporary visas that can be very difficult to get that will allow you to stay here for a limited period of time that you have to renew and be eligible to renew them. In reality, there are just a few different ways to get that green card status, and the only way you can become a US citizen is if you first get the green card status and just get to that point. Then, if you are eligible to have some type of application, our immigration system is totally broken and underfunded. It takes years. We were talking about how a short wait time for a decision on your case is a year, two years. Many of my clients wait for five years or more, and meanwhile they're undocumented or stuck, separated from family members in another country. So, we could have a whole entire panel just on that, but just a brief intro. If everyone else wants to chime in on that.

PARRIS: Another thing is that you need to be sponsored, either by a family member or an employer, which makes it difficult. You can't just come from the outside and just walk in. You need some sort of sponsor there already, which makes it difficult for those that are undocumented because if you need an employer sponsor, generally that takes years and money. If you're a person without skills and are already working, there's really no incentive for the employer to go through that process where by the time they complete it, they may not need you anymore, especially for low-skilled jobs. So, it really does privilege those that are college educated who are applying for jobs at a well-established firm that has the money and sees you as a long-term investment, as opposed to those that are low skilled and coming maybe for seasonal, or maybe just a year because of how long it takes to actually process you. It's just not a lot of incentive to do that, and that then filters everyone towards going the illegal route, because the wait times are long and the bureaucracy is long. There's no incentive for these employers to go through all that.

HERMAN: For me, it's also a personal issue. My wife was undocumented when she was a kid and came here legally. Her parents are Chinese, Taiwanese and started an Italian restaurant in Central Florida. You can imagine how that went. They lost their money, their visa and became undocumented, and then Ronald Reagan came along and said, "You know what, if you have the heart to get here, and you're working hard and not a criminal, there should be a way to fix your papers." So they paid their seventy bucks, and they got green cards, and my wife's a doctor now. Actually, if you look at foreign-born professionals in healthcare it's like twenty-five, thirty percent of all of our doctors are foreign born, and thirty percent, forty percent of our medical researchers are foreign born. I used to work for Michael Bloomberg, and he said our immigration system is national suicide. You couldn't design a worse system than we have right now. It's not driven by sound policy or thinkers. It's driven by political bumper stickers. So, Professor, you mentioned the high skill immigration. Yes, that is a route, but actually that's broken too. We have nationality quotas for our employment-based immigration system, and if you're from China or from India, you could have PhDs, you can have patents, you can have all that kind of stuff, and you might be waiting five or ten years for a green card.

So, Canada is laughing at us and saying, "You guys don't know the new game, the new economy." Talent is the new oil. Drill baby, drill. So, if you're going to inherit someone's education from abroad, they're talented, they've already got their undergrad or masters, you're going to top it off with the PhD, and you're going to say, "Get the hell out of here." That's what we're doing. They go compete against us, go invent the new Google, which was invented by Sergey Brin who came as a refugee as a child from Russia. Go invent new Google, or go invent military technology to harm the United States because that's what we're doing. So, Canada actually comes on US soil to recruit our disgruntled high-skilled immigrants, and say, "Why do you suffer this humiliation?" This country is not valuing innovation and talent from around the world. Actually, Microsoft, when they opened up their R & D in Vancouver fifteen years ago, the press release said, "We're doing this, not because we love Canada. We're doing this because our country won't let us bring in the best of the brains around the world, and we need to be in the same room together." So, our Americans will go across the border to innovate with our international superstars.

On the undocumented side, the last law that we had to legalize the undocumented was 2001. It was called the Life Act, and from the 1980s, the '90s, and early 2000s, we've had a law that said you violated your papers. By the way, forty percent of the undocumented came here legally. They're Canadians, they're British, they're Irish, they're your next-door neighbor. I had a client who was a surgeon at one of the major hospitals in Cleveland, an undocumented immigrant performing on patients. You don't know who they are. Maybe there's somebody here in this room. Forty percent overstayed their visa, but we don't talk about that on the media. Anyway, the last law was the Life Act and it expired April 30, 2001. That law said, "We don't care how you came here, you overstayed, you jumped the wall. We don't care. If you have a sponsor, an employer, or a family member, you pay a thousand dollar fine for the civil violation of violating our precious immigration law, and we're gonna let you move on through. We're going to fingerprint you, make sure you're clean, but if you're going to contribute, you're going to be part of our family." George W. Bush loved that law. He was pushing it at sunset in April 2001. He was pushing for it to be renewed, then September 11 happened, and everything changed, and the war on immigrants began in earnest. "It's us versus them, and they're going to hurt us." So, we got close in 2007 to immigration reform, but then Senator Obama knew that immigration was that rail that you cannot touch if you want to be president of the United States. He backed out of the Senate deal to get immigration reform, and then he didn't make it a priority when he became a president. So, here we are twenty-one years since the Life Act expired, and we don't have a solution, and we don't even know how many people are here without papers. It could be ten million, it could be twenty million. And I posit to our policy makers: Is that a safe situation for America, to have twenty million people running around who are off the grid?

LEE: Thank you for that, thank you for sharing our experiences. I think that perfectly segues into our next question. So with current events such as the busing and flying of immigrants into other states and cities, what more can be done to protect the rights of immigrants and prevent them from being used as political props?

PARRIS: I'm not sure what can be done to prevent it. There are some silver linings—some of these immigrants have been moved from Florida to, say, New York, and many of them are asylum seekers. These court systems in these states are more friendly to their cases, so there is that positive aspect of it. It has highlighted how, because immigration is really a local event, it may be handled at the national level, but it's local institutions that have to integrate them at churches or schools or local ethnic associations. So, it's highlighted how these localities are strained because once they've been sent to New York or Chicago, they have seen how strained the system is. Yeah, they're being used as props for political purposes, and it's not necessarily because—I mean they are strained, you could argue that in Florida or Texas as well, but that's not why they really sent them there. It was election season, and they did that for that reason, but I'm not sure how you prevent it. Unless you can prosecute these states on kidnapping, or I can't remember the other law that I think California is trying to sue for, I think racketeering somehow, but I'm not sure how you prevent it.

But I think it highlights again the problems of dealing with it because we don't really have a formal integration policy. Everything is dealt with at the state level, so if you have a good local system with strong institutions, like good education systems that can handle bilingual students, for instance, or you are in a state that has strong ethnic associations for the population that is predominantly immigrants, then those states do better, but if you don't, then then you don't. So, a lot of new immigrants are coming to the South, for instance. In the South, it's pretty new to immigration because the wave of the early twentieth century skipped the South, and these areas have been really less able to deal with immigrants even though they're sort of the new destination south of the Midwest, but I think it's more highlighting the problems with the system. I'm not sure how you can protect the immigrants from this because there is really no way to protect them.

DROZDA: Yeah, unfortunately I agree with that. It's so upsetting to see what happened in those instances and to feel like there's really not a ton that that can be done, but I think that it's important to understand at least some reasons why the situation at the border is the way it is. The folks that are fleeing and coming to the southern border are painted in the media as if they're doing it illegally, they've snuck across the border, but that virtually doesn't happen anymore. Policies have evolved over the years to make it extremely difficult to sneak across the border. These folks are presenting themselves to border patrol, and they're claiming asylum because there's no incentive to do it any other way, or there's no way to do it a legal route. Asylum is the only option, and that is legal. Our laws say that if you flee your country, and you present yourself here—you can make that brutal journey and make it here—and you say that you fear for your life, by law, you have a right to be put through our immigration system and have an opportunity to request asylum. I think most of the people that are fleeing, just given what they're going through, really are fleeing grave harm and are fleeing for their lives and need protection in the United States. But there are many others that asylum wasn't designed really to address the harms that they have, the needs that they have, the needs that globally we're going to continue to have with climate change, and asylum isn't really designed for those types of needs.

So, you have all these people coming to the border because it's the only way to get here, and when you look at the folks that are there at the border too, talking about how immigration racializes us, they're mostly Black and brown immigrants. In part, because many of the people who are now undocumented, like Richard said, have overstayed their visas. They were able to get some sort of temporary tourist visa to get here. They're mostly white and wealthy immigrants who can prove that they have incentive to go back to their country. That's basically what you have to prove if you want to come here temporarily: look at my life and my country. I have family there, I have a job there, I have money in my bank account, I'm gonna go back. People from the global south, from Central South America, don't often have that to prove. Maybe they'd like to just be able to come temporarily to visit family members or to be able to work temporarily, but they can't get visas. They don't meet those requirements, and they don't have the money to do it. So, you have this huge disparity of folks who are at the border, and then you see the way that they're politicized to meet political gains. So the short answer to that long explanation is that we need reform to be able to protect the rights of immigrants because the situation there is just ripe to be used for political games. It doesn't seem that anyone actually wants to talk about why we have this problem into actually realistically work on solving it.

HERMAN: I'll just add real quick—I get calls almost every day from employers all over the country saying, "I can't find workers," and it's all kinds of jobs. A lot of the back-breaking work that Americans don't want to do, these jobs are just not being filled, and to me it just seems like a logical solution. So, that would help ameliorate some of the pressure if there were avenues like, for example, we have a H-2B visa program for seasonal workers, but it's like a lottery and it's 33,000 for six months, that go... like that. Then, all of a sudden, the shrimp boat industries need more, or the East Coast vacation spots need more, or the Trump Hotel needs more. This is not a way you should be designing a policy. I mean labor market analysis. Where are the holes? How do you fill it? It's not rocket science, so I think that would help ameliorate some of it, but the other part of it is the confusion of our immigration policy is exploited by a lot of different folks and entities, and the word gets out that you can come to the border and apply for asylum. The word should get out that asylum is not for every danger. You could prove that you were going to be killed tomorrow by the cartel if you go back, but that usually doesn't impress an immigration judge. You've got to prove you're likely to be persecuted on account of your political opinion, your ethnic background, your religion, sexual orientation, things like that.

A lot of the stuff that we see in these asylum cases doesn't fit that paradigm. Another thing I mentioned—I think the professor brought up, about the inequities, the disparities between immigration courts. So, here's a good example. I have clients that came in legally, they have a visa, they're at school, and they're like, "I can't go back home." I say, "Okay. Tell me why. Tell me what's going on, and let's figure it out." "Okay, I'm gonna apply for asylum." "Absolutely, you should apply for asylum. Don't do it here. Why? Because you're going to kill your case." It doesn't really matter where you apply at the US immigration level. We have these asylum offices, I think the approval rates are all about the same, if I'm not mistaken, twenty-five percent maybe, approval rates. So, three-quarters of those cases get denied, and if you're out of status at that point, they put you in Immigration Court. That's where you can win your case or lose it, and so in Cleveland—by the way I consider Cleveland to be not an immigrant-friendly city for a lot of different reasons, but the Cleveland Immigration Court is the court that is for all of Ohio. So, all of our immigration cases come here in Cleveland. The approval rate for asylum is probably below fifteen percent. Fifteen percent. If you go to New York City, there are judges that are approving over ninety percent, not just a few—eighty percent, seventy percent, sixty percent. If you are breathing, and you go into that court, you've got a very good chance of getting asylum.

So, why is it that I can go to McDonald's in New York City, and the hamburger will taste the same as LA, but it won't be a political asylum? Why does the law apply in such a disparate fashion? Because it's up to the judges. It's up to their personal politics, their own bias. So when I have people that are getting ready to apply for asylum, we strategically think about what city we can go to live because you can't just say, "I'm living in New York City, and here's my Bronx address." You've got to live there, and a lot of our clients don't have the resources to move to the Bronx. Their family's here, their support system is here, but for many of them, it could help win their case.

PARRIS: The court systems vary just because they're based on those states, so the politics will differ depending on the states, like all our politics differ here subnationally.

KUMAR: Absolutely. That's all very interesting, and I think it really relates to a lot of the conversation around the immigration system today in regard to how often immigrants are politicized and the popular view around immigrants. In general, one such view is that immigrants take away American jobs, take away American labor. We just had that discussion about how immigrants often take jobs that Americans usually don't want or don't take to begin with. Because they're working in these undesired positions from the aspect of US citizens, there are concerns regarding the labor rights of these immigrants, specifically undocumented immigrants. More than just safeguarding the labor rights of immigrants, there's also this question of how can we change this messaging that's very prevalent, this anti-immigrant rhetoric, and how can we push a more pro-immigrant immigration stance, especially when we see maybe more anti-immigrant rhetoric in the media, certain media outlets—I'll let you figure out which ones, but I'll let you take a stab.

PARRIS: I mean, we have a law, although we're known as an immigrant nation, we've hated every immigrant group that's come, every single one. From the Germans, to the Italians, and now the Mexicans, we hate everyone. We say they're going to ruin everything, and generally what has happened is that they become economically integrated or maybe intermarry, and then we move along and hate the next group that comes. So, if history is an example, I think the only way really that you get over the hatred is that you properly integrate them so that the immigrants are part of the economic and relative social mainstream. Like Italians, for instance they were thought of as the bottom of the immigrant barrel in the turn of the twentieth century, but by the time you hit the middle twentieth century, they weren't. I think one difference with the new immigrants post-1960 is that the immigrants from the turn of the twentieth century were from southern Eastern Europe, and originally they were not thought of as white. That was reserved for the northwestern Europeans, and then through intermarriage and economic integration, by the time you get to the middle twentieth century up, it's basically pan-ethnic whiteness. The immigrants from the post-'60s era have been mostly Asians, Africans, Caribbeans, and Latin Americans, and the question is whether or not they can integrate in the same way. I don't think racially—it's not going to be as easy to make them whatever—but they can be integrated economically, which is really about employment and the local economic system in which they're immigrating. That's, to me, the way that you can handle xenophobia, but I don't think there's some magic pill. I mean you can do education. I'm big about pop culture in various ways of softening, normalizing immigrant experiences, but I think if they're economically integrated, not seen as a drag, or stealing somebody's job or problems of crime or whatever, then that's one way that you can bring immigrants into the mainstream and shield them somewhat from integration. But the anti-Asian biases regardless of economic prospects does counter that, so I'm not really sure. Like I said, we've hated every immigrant group, and it's usually only through economic integration that we've sort of stopped hating them.

DROZDA: Yeah, I completely agree with that. I think that it's really at a sort of local, very community-oriented level, and in these times when we're so divided and segregated in our communities, that can be really difficult. So, I do think it's important for local governments, local communities, local organizations to take on that role, to have integration efforts. I love your use of *integration* instead of *assimilation*—notice that's a very important difference. I think that often we talk about how immigrants should assimilate. When I hear that, I think, "Drop all of your practices, your beliefs, and assimilate into whatever our culture is here in the US." Often the de facto is white, European culture, but we have so many cultures, and it's so different from community to community. Integration is much more about what are your backgrounds, your experiences, what do you bring to the community, and how can you work with other different groups in that community to improve the community overall. I think that I've seen a lot more, just in my work, different sort of national organizations that will do trainings on a variety of different things, but I've seen way more trainings than I have in the past on how folks like where I work at Cleveland Legal Aid or other community-based organizations can help to spearhead those integration efforts. So, I think that's a really positive development, that we're talking about more. I think storytelling is really important. We're working with immigrant communities to feel comfortable to tell their stories, and I think the power of storytelling can really help to bring people together. And we realize that we have a lot more in common than we do differences, which I know sounds cheesy, but it's very true. It really just takes those personal connections and maybe an organizing force to facilitate those.

HERMAN: I agree with both those comments. Real quick—I was working on a writing project with Robert Smith, who works here at Case now. He was a *Plain Dealer* reporter at the time, and he was the diversity affairs reporter, and his wife is the first violinist in the Cleveland Orchestra. She's from Korea, and my wife is from Taiwan, so Bob and I are these lazy white guys who would get together and say we can't keep up with our immigrant wives. They have another motor, you know, and they're raising our kids in a way that is different than we were raised. We became friends, and we decided we wanted to write a book together about the positive, because we're troubled that Cleveland was not welcoming immigrants. It welcomed the Eastern European assembly to some degree, although there's always that pushback. But this wave of color, particularly Africans, Asians, Latinos, Arabs—there was a strong, strong xenophobic stench in Cleveland, and I still think it's here today. So we said, "Listen, let's collect stories of immigrants creating jobs, and let's look at this. Let's pull together the recent data on economic contributions." We wanted to catalyze this discussion of post-industrial cities embracing immigration as an economic development strategy, and the data was mind-blowing. Immigrants are twice as likely to start a business than American-born, and that's true whether it's a little bodega or a landscaping company or Silicon Valley. Over half the companies in Silicon Valley were founded by immigrants. Forty percent of the Fortune 500 companies were founded by an immigrant or a child of an immigrant. So, if you look at all those jobs, immigrants are twice as likely to have a patent than an American-born.

I remember going to the City Council testifying to say, "Listen, let's get on the train, let's welcome this wave," because I had some Somali clients that were pushed out. They were trying to set up a taxi company here, and the leadership said no, we don't want them here, and a story that ran in *The New York Times* at that time, fifteen years ago was "Hopkins International Tickets Muslim Drivers for Praying Outside their Cabs." That was the message, and Cleveland wasn't troubled by that at all. It's actually—that's kind of good. So, I was testifying at the City Council, and I said, "Let me drive the bus to Toronto." If you don't believe that a cold industrial city can benefit from immigration, let me show you Toronto. Toronto looked a lot like Cleveland until fifty years ago. Something happened along the way to form it—the world came into Toronto, and Toronto welcomed them. Toronto is now fifty percent foreign born. They have a real estate problem too; they don't have empty houses. They have housing values going four, five, ten, twenty times what it was ten years ago, and the native Toronto folks are saying "not a bad deal." So, to me there's a story to be told, and we did this book. We went around the country interviewing the billionaires, the bodega owners, the immigrant chefs, the medical researchers—from Nigeria or wherever—and the stories were all the same: this is about self-sacrifice, parents investing in their kids, wanting to make their parents proud by working their asses off, and wanting to make something.

And I'll leave you with this: my daughter Isabel was probably three or four years old when Bob and I were working on this book. So, my wife and I were talking about immigration all the time in the house, probably to the point where it was a little bit weird, and our daughter says, "Daddy, Daddy, What's an immigrant?" and I thought, *Well how do you explain this to the Fox crowd at a three-year-old level?* I said, "Honey, immigrants are heroes, and it's like they're in an airplane, and they're gonna jump out, and they're going to try to build this parachute on the way down, and they're doing that for their kids." Now, she didn't understand that, but I'm not sure I do either. But the point was that the message is there. It's a story, if you look at the Congressional Record 1911, 1915, whatever it was—you're so right, Professor, that xenophobia is as American as apple pie and baseball. This is what we do—we hate the newcomers, and then we embrace them, and we wait for the next wave. But that congressional history—I researched it, I pulled it up—these signs of the community, of the business community, of the church communities: "These immigrants coming in, they're ruining this country. They don't speak English, they're criminals, they're bringing in crime, they're taking our jobs, and they're bringing disease." Lou Dobbs said the new wave is bringing leprosy and things like that. So, who is this, who are they talking about in 1915 and 1917? They're talking about the Jews, the Poles, the Italians, the Irish, you know, the Great American generation who fought World War II. So we're going to get through this. I may not be here when it gets right, but you guys will be.

PARRIS: One thing I want to add is it's not only whites that are xenophobic to immigrants coming in, it's actually also people of color or old immigrants who don't like new immigrants. So, it's like a much more complicated xenophobia than simply whites against the new immigrants coming in. It's like African Americans against the new Caribbeans, or Asians against Latinos—it's a multifaceted xenophobia. So in attacking it, I think it's important to acknowledge that. It seems like it's just one Boogeyman against all the masses; it's not like that at all.

HERMAN: Sometimes immigrant communities are very xenophobic themselves, right? So when they come in the boat, and they pull in the ladder after them and say, "Well, we did it the right way, right?" We have friends from Colombia saying, "We did it the right way." Well, what was the right way? "Well, we came here and got a tourist visa when we could get them. We overstayed, it became illegal, and we applied for asylum. We did it the right way." Okay.

LEE: Thank you, thank you for sharing those insights into the American immigration system as a whole, and as a broader picture. We were wondering about that in the media, and generally what we see is that we frequently talk about Latin American immigration into states like California and Texas, but what do you think are the common misconceptions about immigration within Cleveland, Ohio? And so, we kind of talked about this: How does this affect your work that you do, and how does your work in your respective field combat these inequities?

PARRIS: Well, my work focuses on bilingual education at the state level, and teaching immigrants English is probably one of the more important aspects of immigrant integration, but the capacity to do that, they're at the state level, so that's one of the things I was referring to before. This depends on where you go as an immigrant, what kind of services you're going to receive. And since we don't have a truly formal integration policy, it's really about what job you get. Does that job help you? Are there voluntary associations there to aid you in the process of naturalization? Then, is the school system you want to look at equipped? Do they have trained bilingual teachers? Do they fund these programs well enough that they can actually provide not just a two-year bilingual education program, but a five- to seven-year bilingual education program? And all these are really dependent on how invested that locality or state is in funding these things, or if there are voluntary associations that are well-equipped and organized that can do so.

So, with Cleveland—I don't really do work in Cleveland, but I know with the rejection of immigrants coming here was the African American Community saying, "We don't want immigrants here," even though immigrants would help revitalize the city by bringing in jobs and employment and entrepreneurship, and all this would benefit everybody. But to me it's about educating everybody that immigrants aren't going to steal from you, and I can see why. There's a long history of African Americans being threatened by immigration and some rightfully so. Like the turn-of-the-century immigrants were always preferred over African Americans when they were migrating North during The Great Migration, so there's a history for that resentment that is real, but rejecting them from here was probably horribly self-destructive, because the city is aging, and there's a depopulation in Cleveland, and the cities that are vibrant are the ones that have immigrants. So it's really understanding that people aren't coming to take, which, it's like you said, as American as apple pie, but they're coming to revitalize. I think that's a multi-form education effort to get people to understand that. You can't just tell people—you can't just yell at people—you kind of have to see where they're coming from and speak with them or get them to see things for what they are, instead of these kinds of strong-man stereotypes.

HERMAN: So, I used to love reading about what makes a city immigrant-friendly, and then I got so depressed reading these things. I had one billionaire in town, I won't tell you who, call me up and said, "Shut the f up. Stop talking about immigration in Cleveland. You're going to create a race war." So, I think he had visions of Hough on fire in the 1960s. Rather than saying, "Why don't we build those new relationships in a way that's not threatening because the data is not going to sell anybody—it's about building these relationships and trust," which I think is happening in other cities, but they're not willing to buy it here. But I think immigrant-friendly cities have a lot of common characteristics, and even Rust Belt cities now. I'm not talking about cities that have a huge percentage of immigrants; we're only 5 percent foreign-born in Cleveland. The national average is probably 12 or 13 percent. Cities that are economically popping are twenty, 25 percent or higher, so we're very low in the immigrant population, but I think a lot of them have things like an immigrant welcome center, a coalition, one place where you can go for your ESL, and you can get resource referrals and all this kind of stuff. By the way, most of those that are effective are in City Hall. In Boston, I don't know if it still is, but it was Mayor Menino when he was the mayor, I went to visit, he goes "I want that office in in city hall right next to me," and I was there for Christmas time, and he said "are you coming to the party for Christmas?" and I said, "What party?" and he said, "We're having a diversity party." I said, "That sounds like a great idea." So I think that once you start to say, "I want to become an immigrant-friendly city, you start to see all these different policies that can come out," for example IDs, a city ID. If the feds don't want to give us an ID or a driver's license, maybe the city can, and that could at least get us into the library, and I think it's a formal acknowledgment that you're part of us, we don't care about your papers, you're a member of our community.

Again, if you start digging, you start really seeing the layers of the onion, you could be in the Chamber of Commerce and you could say "I want Congress to push for immigrant-friendly destinations to reboot economically-deprived cities." What does that mean? Well we have an H-1B visa for professional workers, for those techies I was talking about in Silicon Valley that are leaving for Canada. We have this lottery system. There's only 85,000 of these visas per year, so Facebook, Microsoft, they're all vying for these. It's a lottery, and the visas go instantaneously. Hundreds of thousands of people apply within a week's span, then they're gone. So why don't we create a situation where if you move your company into Cleveland or Detroit, you can get relief from the lottery, you don't need the lottery to hire those folks if you co-locate those jobs here. Because right now, Microsoft and other companies are setting up those jobs over the border in Canada—it's called *near-shoring*. Do it in Cleveland. Create jobs and revenue here. We have investment green cards—if you invest money in economically deprived areas and create ten jobs, you get green cards. We don't really hear too much about that. I was advocating for that use in Hough in our inner-city areas. You don't hear about that. So again, I think if you ask the question, "Do you want to be an immigrant-friendly city?," you're going to see all these discussions roll out, and the problem with Cleveland is we haven't asked that question yet.

DROZDA: Can I just add, briefly in my work, misperceptions about immigration to Cleveland. Just sort of generally speaking, I see a lot of the same misperceptions that we see nationally, in terms of how our immigration system works and immigrants that are here, why they're here, and how they got here, and all those things that we've already covered. But another thing I've seen is that we don't have any immigrants here. We have talked about how Cleveland could definitely be more immigrant friendly. But I think a lot of people are surprised to learn that my clients are not just from Mexico and Central America, but from many, many different countries. What I see is the work that I do at Cleveland Legal Aid and my colleagues is working with our clients to bring stability and security to their lives so that they can integrate more into the community and dispel some of those misperceptions and contribute and thrive. The first step for me is, of course, they come and they have questions about their immigration status, and figuring out what they qualify for, what can we apply for, and we kind of go from there. Making referrals within Legal Aid, we assist with housing, employment issues, education issues—so it's never just the immigration cases, it's often troubleshooting many other problems to provide security for families that we serve. I think a great example of that is that we have, for the past six months or so, we received a grant to provide immigration legal services to Afghans who've been resettled here that fled Afghanistan in August 2021, after the US forces withdrew, and around a thousand Afghans have been resettled here in Cleveland. Legal Aid and Catholic Charities, together, we're handling the legal cases for all of those families. So that has just been a great example of connecting them with resources, and I just I've never worked with a population that has literally been just more new; everything is new. They know nothing here, and so it's been a really great experience to welcome them to Cleveland and try to step-by-step—it will take many, many years, but to integrate them into our community, and I think that will be a really positive contribution to Cleveland in years to come, hopefully.

KUMAR: Well, clearly we have a long way to go, but it is nice to hear that steps are being taken to address some of these issues, regardless of how impossible they may seem to address initially. So, moving on to our individual questions we're going to ask—if you guys don't mind, of course—each panelist, individually, a question. Of course any one of you can jump in if you'd like, but starting with Miss Drozda. Now, obviously many of the people coming to this country have very limited English competency. They're coming from all over the world, so obviously you can't always expect these people to understand or know English. My question is then how can the immigration process be changed so that those of limited English competency can be more adequately represented and supported throughout the immigration process?

DROZDA: That's a great question. Definitely a huge need. First of all, none of the immigration applications are in any languages other than English, which is crazy. How can you fill something out that's very complicated in English if you're an immigrant who has just arrived here? Just to illustrate, I think the best example of that is I occasionally represent folks who are in removal proceedings and are in detention, so they're in civil immigration detention and sometimes, for a variety of reasons, have to stay in detention during their entire removal proceedings. I don't always provide full-on representation, but try to help them through that process. They're extremely isolated, they don't have a lot of access to, or funds available to have people to help them do that. They don't have a very basic library with limited time to be able to do that. And it's like here's this fifteen-page asylum application form that requires like narrative answers. I mean how is someone supposed to do that? So, sometimes we've had cases that we've gotten because someone tried to represent themselves in Immigration Court and filled out the form as best they could in their native language, and the immigration judge is like, "No, you have to fill this out in English." The question is, How do I do that? "Like I don't know, figure it out!" So I guess step one would be, there should be forms available in languages, and the Immigration Court, the system, the other immigration agencies should accept those and use their resources to have those translated. It's all on the applicant to translate all their documents into English, to submit everything in English, and that's extremely difficult to do if you don't have an attorney. I will say, the immigration courts are pretty good at providing interpreters for people who are in immigration proceedings, so that's positive—a lot better than some of our local Cleveland and Ohio courts that are not immigration related—but I think that would be a huge benefit to be able to have those forms translated.

And just one other thing I'll mention is for people who are coming at the border and are being given all of these documents, saying "Okay now you're going to be put in removal proceedings, you're going to go here, if you don't show up at this report date, or if you don't show up at this hearing you're going to be ordered removed" And all this is in English! Sometimes the form will say, "Oh this was read to this person in Spanish" But I'm pretty confident it's never by a qualified interpreter. It's just whatever the border official—maybe they can speak Spanish, but if it's another language, they don't have officers who speak the many other languages of people or who are coming in. So much, much better language access, at the border would be a huge step in the right direction.

LEE: Awesome. Thank you, thank you. So another question that we had, and this one's for Professor Parris. So we mentioned immigrant integration. How does immigrant immigration balance preservation of unique cultures while encouraging and bringing immigrants into American society? How do we find that equilibrium? How do we find that balance where we can adequately support these immigrants? Thank you.

PARRIS: It's a good question. I think the fact that we don't have a formal integration process almost creates the balance. So we do push immigrants to learn English and then generally their integration happens through their job. But the other entity that plays a role in integration are usually ethnic associations. Generally immigrants integrate through their communities. Whether it's ethnic association or family, I think that creates a fairly decent balance. The real key is that, in terms of integrating economically, they're not segmented into these jobs that are low skilled and have only immigrants where they kind of stay there. If there's a way, maybe not that generation, but the next generation, through education, can then move on to higher types of employment that have a wider variety of persons. Because generally when immigrants come, they come to some sort of economic immigrant enclave through a job. But if in a generation you can move on, I think you can balance that because basically the immigrant community integrates you, and the sort of the economic aspect further integrates you into the American mainstream. I think you can score that balance that way. I don't think you have to really do anything, as long as there's not—as you were mentioning—the assimilation. So in the early twentieth century, we were forcing assimilation onto immigrants because they were seen as a danger. Right after World War I, it was backlash against immigrants, and they needed to be Americanized. But we've kind of moved away from that, and it's really much more on the ethnic communities. And so if you can balance the economic while still integrating through the ethnic community, I think you can score a nice balance.

KUMAR: So our last question is for you, Mr. Herman. And it relates to something that a lot of students, especially international students have to deal with, and that's the student visa process. So the question in particular is how does the student visa process compare with someone seeking employment in the United States?

HERMAN: I think most students don't have a problem getting the student visa, but that's not always true depending on what country you're coming from and what program you're coming to study at. For example, if you're coming from the Philippines to study at a community college in Cleveland, you probably have a high denial rate, as opposed to coming from China, depending on what university in China, coming for an advanced degree in the United States. So the student visas I don't think are the problem. I do a lot of counseling of international students getting ready to graduate and enter into the job market, and you've got to have a war plan. I mean, you've got to have multiple layers of strategy if this doesn't work. So, the first thing is when you graduate you get OPT (optional practical training). If you're a STEM grad, you can get several year extensions, and that's really cool because your employer doesn't have to file anything. But also, you've got to be careful because employers could be predatory if they don't have to pay prevailing market wage when you're on OPT. The biggest asset that a student can have in marrying with an employer—it's a marriage—is you want to pick the one that is likely to apply for your H-1B visa—that lottery that I talked about—and likely if they win the lottery, even if they don't, likely to apply for a green card for you. And these processes take years sometimes, so you also don't pick the first employer that's kind of cute and winks at you. You've got to do your due diligence and so, for example, there's a website called myvisajobs.com. It's a private website. You gotta pay a little money to get on, and I have no ownership interest in that. But it takes the data from the Department of Labor and aggregates it so you can do searches to see which employers have filed H-1Bs, which college degrees they're hiring, who signed the H-1B petition from the employer, what city they're in. You can also see which companies are filing for green cards, because they've got to file labor certification applications to prove they're not displacing an American worker. That data is extremely valuable because now you know this company is immigrant friendly, they're filing H-1Bs. They know what that is, they know about international human capital strategies, they're deploying them, the HR person is not scared when they hear the word immigration.

Secondly, they file green cards, some employers will say "We'll file H-1Bs, but we don't do the green cards." So you don't want to invest years of your life with an employer H-1B and find out they don't do the green cards, because that green card process can take years and years and years. For my Indian friends, it could take ten years. And we have all kinds of brainstorming sessions on how to play that strategy out, so the bottom line is develop a strategy early on in your college career about finding the right employer that's going to be immigrant friendly and sponsor you because it's going to be very, very valuable for you down the road.

KUMAR: Thank you, all three of you, for answering these questions. And going back to the topic of students, we're now going to open up the floor to any questions any of you might have. There's a microphone right over there if everyone can direct their attention to where I'm pointing.

AUDIENCE: Sorry, I had to write it down. So, speaking in the realm of political asylum today with the shifting of the migrant body to represent truth. I've heard about medical examiners refusing to do asylum evaluations or lawyers recommending their clients against using pornography to prove queerness. Is there a way to push back against these really violent expectations without disenfranchising current migrants in their processes that you've come across?

DROZDA: That's a really interesting question, and something I think about. Not necessarily that specific example, but I think about a lot how to really value your clients experiences and empower them in telling their story, but you also have to you want them to win, so you have to keep in mind who the audience is. So, it is a really difficult balance. I try my best to be mindful of that and think about *Am I phrasing this in this way for this reason* or *Why do I think about it like that*, but I think it is difficult because you also come across different grounds of inadmissibility, so different reasons why someone—and that's a little bit different in asylum—there are different types of bars to reasons why someone is just not eligible for what they're applying for. So, you have to be really careful and constantly be thinking, is saying this gonna lead us down the rabbit hole of all these questions. A government prosecutor, if it's in a removal proceedings situation, is going to ask all these horrible, terrible questions that are just really going to break your client down. You constantly have to be thinking of all of these different things, and it's really a conversation with your client, to be honest, but it can be like a fine line.

HERMAN: Just to add to that. I mean it's really important to develop that trust with the client because sometimes they don't know what question should be asked or what I'm asking really is. I'll give you a concrete example. So, I have one client I represented, a company, and they called me up, and they said, "We've got a young lady from El Salvador. She's being deported next week. She's been ordered, deported, she's been through the process, Immigration Court she's got this whole, she's done, and she's got to report to ICE next Wednesday." I said, "Okay, I don't know what I could do, but I'll be happy to talk with her." So, I talked to her and she was like, twenty-one years old, twenty-two years old. I just had a sense we should dig deeper, and so I said, "Why don't you talk to one of the lawyers in my office, someone else." The lawyer that I was thinking about was Charmaine. I said, "Why don't you talk to Charmaine in private," and it turns out that this young girl was living with her mom here. Her mom's undocumented too. The mom's boyfriend made the young girl quit high school to go work, and then he took her paychecks. She didn't think anything of it. I said that sounds like labor trafficking. So, we contacted the ICE officer. We said, "We're filing for the T-VISA for trafficking." Usually, you see the trafficking cases on sex trafficking and sometimes labor trafficking, and this is not really your traditional labor trafficking, but it meets the definition. So the ICE officer says, "Well let's meet at McDonald's—again that McDonald's, I don't know why everybody wants a Big Mac. So we meet at McDonald's, kind of a weird place to meet, and he's like, "Are you sure?" I said, "Yeah," the lawyers in me, but I said, "Yeah, we're sure. We're gonna file this." "Okay, okay, I'll give you some time to explore." We ended up winning that case.

So, you know, I have a lot of LGBT clients. They're applying for asylum, sexual orientation-based cases. I remember when Janet Reno was the attorney general and sexual orientation became grounds for asylum. It's really historic. We started doing cases, and it's just a matter of trying to develop trust and dialogue with your client because they may not even tell their lawyer what's really happening, and you got to really get it out, and then you make the judgment call. Is it going to help or hurt the case?

DROZDA: I'll just add really briefly as well. I think another thing too, is it's really important to educate the adjudicator. So, I'm thinking of a case now. It's a woman in removal proceedings. She identifies as lesbian, but we have a multi-faceted claim because people are complicated, not everyone fits into one hole and one little box. An immigration judge—and I know who this judge is, it's a white man—would very much like for it to fit into this one box, but we have a domestic violence-based claim. She was with a male partner that she has children with. So I'm already thinking this is going to be a tough case, but she needs to tell her story, so we're gonna just have to educate the judge and do the best that you can while valuing your clients experiences, and making sure she has the chance to request the relief that she deserves.

AUDIENCE: Sorry, one more quick, just, sub-part of that. Again, with research and evidence into nowadays, with necropolitics and violence and waiting, Do you think there's realistically a lot of value in, beyond just a research sense, in applying these experiential evidences in a system of doubt?

HERMAN: I'm not sure I understand your question.

AUDIENCE: Oh, just given that the whole political asylum system is all based on realistically doubting and trying to find flaws. Now, there's research saying, well, the system is bad for migrants, it puts them in these bad positions. Their existence is being taunted with this spot between life and death, but it's all really experiential, and I guess if they were not believing migrants already, is this experiential evidence really doing much?

DROZDA: Hmm, I don't know. I'm not sure how to answer that question. Yeah, I don't know. I mean I'll just add, I mean, the asylum process is definitely brutal. You know, you're really put through the wringer, and our entire immigration system is definitely does not have trauma in mind or really anything like that, and I think we're constantly fighting against that.

HERMAN: I think it comes down to storytelling. So, a good lawyer is a good storyteller, and you've got to know your audience—or like Sun Tzu, know your enemy. You've got to be able to give them the opportunity, to give them the hook, to say okay, now I see that the law meets the facts and I can approve it. So, the first thing you've got to do is get the story out of the client, and that's not always easy because they may have trauma, they may have language or cultural issues, trust issues, so getting the story out. Usually I ask them, I say write it down please, and don't worry about grammar. You don't have to be Dostoevsky, just give me the story. So, if you can't write it, get someone to help you write it, or maybe we can help you write it in your language, or want to translate it. Get the story. Once we have the story, then we can start seeing the case kind of materialize. For example, not a lot of clients have the resources for this, but I love to get expert witnesses, country experts. If we can find a PhD—we have another one here, a PhD who is an expert on this one issue—we'll go to him or her and say, "Hey, we've got somebody, can you evaluate the case and issue an expert opinion? In my humble opinion, based on my research and evaluation of this case, this person will suffer persecution." Persecution is a legal term, so that's what the judge looking for. Are we hitting the legal notes? If the person suffered trauma, have we documented the trauma? If it's physical injury, do we have medical reports? If it's psychological injury, can we afford a forensic psychologist report, or at least some other type of medical professional to evaluate trauma? Judges appreciate that. I think you mentioned people who are detained. Only ten percent of detainees have counsel, ten percent have lawyers. So, the judges by and large do appreciate when a lawyer is there and they're properly prepared.

The case is prepared; there's documents there. We have the country reports, but the bottom line of your question is if it's just your story that is going to be enough, and the law says, yes as long as the judge does not think there's other documents that you could have gotten. If you say this happened to me and there were witnesses and you don't explain why you don't have witness statements like my mom was right there, where's Mom's statement? Can she email it to you, can she fax it to you? You've got to give them something because a lot of people don't present that stuff. They just go there with their story, and the judge is like you know—there is a lot of fraud. I mean in the immigration system, there's marriage fraud, there's document fraud. It's real, so I don't want to just demonize the other side and say, you know—people do make stuff up. So, to the degree that they can, the client and their team has to document their claim.

AUDIENCE: One of my first questions is when you were talking about how the immigrants take the jobs that Americans don't want. My problem with that is because me and my mother are refugees, but my brother and sister were born here, and my mother's accepted the jobs that she works are the jobs that Americans don't really want, and those are where the places where there's a lot of hiring and stuff, but then there's also like a lot of dangers in those jobs and the payments. The salaries, they're not up to par with how hard those jobs are and—. It's like where's the ethics in that? How is someone that is just working on the computer all day making more than someone that's doing physical labor, and they work overtime. Sometimes, they don't get paid for that overtime, and they maybe they get like a salary increase every year, but it's cents, it's not really doing anything, and with the inflation rates every year, the salary and the inflation rates, well they never equal each other. Basically I'm just saying, Why are like the immigrants or the refugees or migrant workers here not getting paid like other Americans are getting paid? They're not really incentivized to unionize or join a union because unions take money out of your paychecks, and you have places for where your money should go because you don't have a foundation in this country, so you can't be throwing your money anywhere willy-nilly. We don't really take out loans or anything because we see what it does to other people. So we're not really incentivized to do what the government says—oh do this, apply for this—it's like no because we know that the American government will always find a way to get their money back. If you apply for welfare, then they'll just take that much money out of your next income taxes, and it's always somehow to get you trapped in this thing. So, why isn't there a good system for immigrants to just set a foundation in this country?

PARRIS: I would say that you need to unionize and that unionization shouldn't be seen as wasting money— that unionization and collectively organizing is the way that you can have collective leverage to raise your salaries because the industry does not want to pay you. Industries don't want to pay anybody if they can get away with it. I mean the idea with profit is that you produce something with the least cost that would be exploiting your labor as much as possible. Sounds Marxist, but, yeah, whatever. So, I would say that unionization is not a waste of money, that is actually a relatively—I mean not maybe long-term—but an investment in boosting your income because as an individual, especially as an immigrant, you don't have any leverage. You're seen as at the bottom, and the only way that you can get good wages is through unionization. That's the early—from the Franklin Delano Roosevelt era, those unions were all immigrants, but that was a focus of the Democratic Party at that time, of collectively organizing labor so that they could have leverage against what we're seeing as exploitive industry. So I would say unionization is the route to go. That's the only way, because you're not gonna incentivize the employers to pay because they just won't.

DROZDA: I think that's the problem with capitalism, yeah.

HERMAN: I would also add that keeping the status quo on undocumented immigration is a boon for a lot of employers. I have people calling me saying, "Well, I got injured at work. I don't want to make a workers' comp claim because I'm undocumented." She talked about doing dangerous jobs and things like that. So, we've got to bring people out of the shadows. For example, we have a system called E-Verify. Employers can now volunteer to go into the system and be registered with the federal government so we can verify every worker's ability to be here lawfully and work. It's so simple, but it's voluntary. Why is it voluntary? Because the politicians and the companies don't want to be required to sign up because right now if you go to apply for a job and you're undocumented, you may have a fake green card. It looks real, and under the law, all the employers have to do is look at it and go, "Looks real," and that's it. Are you kidding me? In this day of technology, we can't run that document through a system and verify? We don't want to know.

By the way, when ICE, Immigration Customs Enforcement, come in for a raid of an employer—which they usually don't do nowadays—the biggest fines that I see to the employers are for not having their I-9s filled out, that small form that everyone fills out including Americans when you get a job. The biggest fines are not for hiring undocumented immigrants. The biggest fines are for not filling out that crappy little piece of paper for Americans, big fines, thousands and thousands of dollars.

AUDIENCE: Also, I have a question about, I forget which one of you spoke on it, but about the translating issues that if it's not Spanish or English, it's over for you. But also I would like to add on how some languages that are spoken are not standardized language like they learned in school. What they're speaking and writing and reading is not just purely that language. For instance, in my culture some of our languages are a mixture of other languages. I know that when my mother used to get translators, they would give her a translator that only knew the base language and everything in that language, but it wasn't really culturally our language, and they never allowed me to translate for her because they said, "Oh she's a child. She can't translate for you." It would just be difficult for her because the people didn't really want to listen to her because they'd be like, "Oh we can't understand you," but she was responding to everything they were saying. They just were being ignorant because her accent was different, so they wanted to act like they did not understand what she was saying. But it was very clear what she was saying, and it was just taunting her because she wasn't saying it in their accent. I was there, and they rejected to use me because they said I was a child. So, if you can't use your relative or your kid to translate for you, then how are you going to get a translator that will perfectly try to tell the other person what you're saying?

DROZDA: You bring up a really important problem. I think just in terms of using family members as interpreters, it is not best practice to do that because depending on the circumstance, an interpreter should be a neutral person who's just there to be able to be basically take the place of the person who's speaking the other language and convey that directly. There might be things, depending on the situations, that your mom might have not felt comfortable with you having to be able to interpret for her because we are close to our family members, you know? Sometimes, it's much easier to say difficult things to someone that you don't know that has no connection to you than the people that you care about the most. I'm someone who with clients or in other situations always discourages family members being used as interpreters, especially children for that reason. But I can say, at least in our work, if we know that there's a specific dialect of a language that's spoken in one part of the country—Spanish, for example, is very different between the Dominican Republic and in Mexico—we really try to find an interpreter that speaks that specific dialect. If I'm going to use this interpreter for an important interview, I often have my client talk with the interpreter ahead of time and practice to make sure that they understand each other. Sometimes we do change, but in a context where you're not working with your attorney or someone who's willing to search and find that perfect interpreter, it is a huge problem. I completely agree, and you are at a huge disadvantage, so that's really frustrating, really difficult for sure.

LEE: So, thank you again to our amazing panelists for taking the time to come out and talk with us about these issues. There are many different avenues to find solutions to improve our immigration system and to achieve a more equitable society that incorporates existing solutions that have been highlighted here as well as emerging policies.

KUMAR: I've been waiting to do that all night, so. All right, so with that, this panel discussion is now closed. The Global Ethical Leaders Society would like to give some thanks to our advisor Beth Trecasa for all that she's done—

[*Applause*]

KUMAR: —and Dr. French—I certainly didn't forget about you. So we would like to give a big round of applause to Dr. French.

[*Applause*]

KUMAR: In addition, we want to thank the Media Vision staff for assisting us with the setup and logistical support here in the Moot Courtroom as well as the various GELS members who helped with setting up this event, the planning committee. In particular—he wasn't expecting this—I would really like to thank Mr. Fred Lee here for doing all that he did to help set up this event. He really pulled through for us, and we're all very thankful. I would also like to give a massive round of applause—well not just me of course, I would hope you all join me—to our amazing panelists for joining us here and discussing all of these important issues with us tonight. So, thank you very much.

[*Applause*]

Killing the Black Body
The Urgency of Reproductive Justice
October 11, 2022

Dorothy E. Roberts
George A. Weiss University Professor of Law & Sociology, Raymond Pace & Sadie Tanner Mossell Alexander Professor of Civil Rights, Professor of Africana Studies & Director, Penn Program on Race, Science & Society, University of Pennsylvania
Colette Ngana
doctoral candidate, Department of Sociology, Case Western Reserve University, and Chair, Board of Directors, Preterm

NGANA: Good morning, thank you all for joining us today. My name is Colette Ngana, and my pronouns are she/her. I'm a doctoral candidate in the department of Sociology here at Case Western, and I also chair the board of directors at Preterm, which is a nonprofit abortion clinic here in Cleveland. I'm just going to be guiding a conversation today with Professor Roberts, so I'm going to do a brief introduction, and then we can get started with our conversation. Professor Roberts is the 14th Penn Integrates Knowledge Professor and George A. Weiss University Professor of Law and Sociology at the University of Pennsylvania. She also holds appointments in the Departments of Africana studies, Sociology, and the Law School, where she is the Inaugural Raymond Pace and Sadie Tanner Mossel Alexander professor of Civil Rights.

Dorothy Roberts is also the founding director of the Penn Program on Race, Science, and Society—an internationally recognized scholar, public intellectual, and social justice advocate; she has written and lectured extensively on race, gender, and class inequities in US institutions and has been a leader in transforming public thinking and policy on reproductive freedom, child welfare, and bioethics. Dorothy Roberts is a prolific scholar and is the author of *Killing the Black Body: Race, Reproduction, and the Meaning of Liberty*, among other books. She has also published more than one hundred articles and book chapters including "Race," in *The 1619 Project* book. So if everyone could join me in welcoming Professor Roberts, that would be great, thank you.

[*Applause*]

NGANA: Well first, how are you?

[*Laughter*]

ROBERTS: I'm doing very well, thank you. It's wonderful to see you, and I'm sorry I can't be there in person. I'm in Cincinnati, where I just gave a talk, and I couldn't get there in time, but I'm glad I can join you all remotely anyway.

NGANA: Perfect. Thank you so much. So I have a few questions prepared already. We're hoping that maybe we can have some audience participation too if there's time that allows, so I guess we can get started. In the articles and books that you've written, you've made compelling arguments for us to move away from the language of reproductive choice and focus efforts instead on reproductive justice. So why is using a justice instead of a rights framework important?

ROBERTS: It's important because it's the only way to oppose the oppressions that are enacted in the name of reproduction and population control—the kinds of violences that people have experienced targeting their reproductive lives rooted in white supremacy, racism, classism, disability injustice, and other kinds of societal inequities. Choice doesn't capture those, and rights don't fully capture what we need in order to have true reproductive freedom. So choice in particular, which has been the predominant way of framing reproductive freedom by mainstream reproductive rights organizations for a long time—also a way of framing it in most jurisprudence—privileges people who have the most power, the most access, who are the most valued in our society, and who can make choices. Rights tend to focus on protecting those choices from government interference, but they don't take into account the structural factors that make it impossible for many people to make choices. They also don't take into account the way in which we may need protection from the government or we may need affirmative resources provided by the government. So both because most constitutional interpretations of rights are negative and because they don't take into account the structural inequities, the power imbalances that have the most impact on our lives and produce the most inequality, the frameworks of choice and rights are limited. I would say that choice is not only unhelpful, it puts us at a disadvantage because it sets up a framework where if you end up being oppressed, you end up having limitations on your freedom, on your autonomy, the comeback is, "Well, you made bad choices." It focuses so much on the individual, as if individuals have freedom as long as the government isn't banning them from doing something, when in fact there are all sorts of societal pressures that deny freedom. Also, it doesn't take into account the devaluation of certain people's choices, so that even when the government prohibits them or punishes them for making decisions, society doesn't always recognize it because it doesn't value their decisions.

So we can talk about this some more, but just so this doesn't sound so abstract, Black women's reproduction has been devalued. Our autonomy over our bodies has been devalued since the time of slavery and even after emancipation. Our childbearing has been devalued, so policies that regulate our reproduction have been treated as good for society. And so it doesn't even seem as if it's a reproductive violation. For example, take enacting welfare laws that deter people from having children. Many people think that's good because they don't recognize how these laws are fueled by stereotypes about Black reproduction and and the view that Black childbearing is dangerous and should be controlled.

Reproductive justice includes the affirmative human right to have a child or not have a child, which includes the right to abortion. As I was emphasizing, this means not just the right against government interference but also the right to public support. We can see after the Dobbs decision, the importance of having a constitutional right to abortion, but that was never enough if you couldn't afford one. The Supreme Court held soon after Roe v. Wade that there was no constitutional right to public funding for abortion. So we were already from the beginning without a true right to terminate a pregnancy. Reproductive justice also includes the human right to have a child and to have a child under the conditions that you want, which includes birth justice. Again you have to have the means to have a child and then also, what is often neglected—the right to parent your child in a safe community with the conditions that are required to be able to take care of a child. The economic, social, and political conditions. That your children are valued by society and your family is supported and not experiencing devaluation and violence against it. So all of these are essential to true reproductive freedom, which Black women in particular have been at the forefront of advocating for for centuries. I think it's wrong to think of our advocacy for reproductive justice as just being recent and a reaction to a reproductive rights or choice framework. It's been deeply part of Black feminist thinking and activism for a very long time.

NGANA: So in that answer you mentioned a few policy level restrictions. You mentioned the recent ruling of Dobbs, which effectively overturned Roe v. Wade, leaving abortion up to the states. So we went back to the states' rights, which is what it was previously, as well as the funding restrictions that we have through policies like the Hyde Amendment. So I'm going to ask you a question on some of your work that follows these legislative policies. When you first wrote *Killing the Black Body*, it was in the wake of legislative moves rooted in these systems that you were talking about: racism, sexism, classism, and the stereotypes that were used to increase the criminalization of pregnancy and limit social support services. Ultimately the goal was to lower fertility, specifically among certain populations which include Black and poor people, but today we're seeing this continued push through policies like Dobbs to control and limit reproductive rights, specifically abortion rights. If you could speak a little bit about the trajectory that you've seen in policy from when you wrote *Killing the Black Body* in the 1990s to today. It's a pretty big gap of time, but if you can give us a little glimpse.

ROBERTS: Well, you could have asked for the trajectory since 1619, and I could answer that as well. I think it is interesting that all of what we're talking about today can be traced back to the exploitation of Black women's reproductive labor during the institution of slavery. Maybe we'll get to that as well, but starting from the late 1980s, early 1990s, that was when I began to notice the prosecutions of women for being pregnant and using drugs. I immediately thought, I bet these are mostly Black women who are being punished this way, and I thought of it as the punishment of Black women for being pregnant. They weren't being punished for drug use. They were being punished for being pregnant and using drugs. Drug use was just one mechanism for punishing them for their pregnancies. I wrote about it as the way in which the intersection of racism and sexism, and also the War on Drugs turned a public health issue of drug use during pregnancy into a crime. For the first time, women were being prosecuted for their conduct during pregnancy. Before the late 1980s, there weren't prosecutions of women for being pregnant and using drugs. Of course this was all fomented and fueled by the myth of the so-called "crack baby," who was treated as if they were monsters who were predicted to not be able to learn, to become criminals, to become welfare cheats, and become a huge burden on US society from the minute of birth, all of which has been discredited and was racist mythology from the very beginning. These kinds of claims were never made about other babies who might have been exposed to drugs in the womb. Now, I was arguing then—along with others in the reproductive justice movement—that we had to pay attention to the punishment of pregnant people, people who wanted to have babies and that this was connected to restrictions on abortion. Remember at the time, most of the reproductive rights movement was focused on legal abortion and preserving Roe v. Wade, but there initially was not the same kind of outcry against these prosecutions, which were related to a long history of reproductive violence against Black women, during the same period of the 1990s.

Not only was the media circulating the myth of the pregnant Black crack addict and the myth of the crack baby, but also the myth of the Black welfare queen, that Black women were having babies just to get a welfare check and that they were then spending the money on themselves and neglecting their children. So, as we're seeing the rise of these prosecutions, we're also seeing advocacy for ending the federal guarantee of welfare, which had been assumed for decades. Now, there was a push to end welfare and to allow states to put restrictions on welfare receipts that included what's called child exclusion policies or family caps—denying additional welfare benefits to people who already are on welfare when they get pregnant and have another child. Those restrictions were intended to deter welfare recipients from having more children. So we see in the 1990s the prosecutions which were punishments for having children. We see the end of the federal guarantee to welfare. We see the build-up of criminal law enforcement—the 1994 Violent Crime Control and Law Enforcement Act was passed in the same period, again fueled by negative images about Black women having dangerous children. I'll mention one other law because I think all this is related, and it shows the intersections of these policies that have been fueled by these same negative stereotypes and carceral logics. One year after the welfare restructuring law was passed, Congress enacted the 1997 Adoption and Safe Families Act, which was supposed to deal with the huge foster care population. At the time, the largest group of children in foster care were Black children. Black children were four times as likely to be taken from their families and put in foster care as white children. The Adoption and Safe Families Act sped up termination of parental rights, perceived as Black mothers rights to their children, and incentivized states to increase the adoptions of children out of foster care instead of returning them home. To sum this up, we can see the intersection of policies that are about reproductive injustice: Policies to criminalize pregnancies, policies to restrict abortion, policies to change welfare into a behavior modification system, and policies to increase the separation of children from their families. All of these are reproductive injustices whose connections went largely unseen at the time. Think about the fallout of the Dobbs decision, what that is going to mean for people's health, for their autonomy over their bodies, for their freedom over their lives, for their ability to raise their families in healthy and safe conditions. Although it's an extremely precarious position, we can now see more clearly these connections and the need to come together in the various movements that are addressing them to form a stronger reproductive justice movement connected to movements for economic justice, connected to movements for environmental justice, for gender justice, for family justice, for birth justice—they are all connected.

NGANA: Yeah, thank you. I think this also brings up, just in the recent policies that we have, we've criminalized pregnancy in ways of not being able to travel across state lines. States have laws like that, associated with restricting the needs that people have around health care, so you can see how this criminalization that you're referencing is building over time and becoming different depending on how these policies are written. You mentioned the child welfare system as connected to the trajectory that we're experiencing, and I was wondering if you could tell us a little bit more about your recent work and how it relates to the conversation we're having today.

ROBERTS: My latest book that was published in April 2022 is called *Torn Apart: How the Child Welfare System Destroys Black Families and How Abolition Can Build a Safer World*. It focuses on what's called the child welfare system, foster care, child protective services. I'm calling it a family policing system because it's based in accusing family caregivers for harming their children, then investigating them, regulating their families, often separating them from their children, putting children in foster care, then supervising them, and in many cases terminating the rights of family members to be a legal family. It is based on the idea that the harms to children are caused by their parents and other family caregivers and the way to address the unmet needs of children is to blame their families and take children away or threaten to take them away.

As I mentioned earlier, one of the key three tenets of reproductive justice is the right to parent your child and to parent your child in a community that has the resources it needs to meet children's needs. Most of the children who are taken from their families by this system are taken on grounds of neglect. About eighty percent of the children taken are taken on grounds of neglect.

Only about sixteen percent are removed because of child abuse whether physical or sexual child abuse. Neglect is typically confused with poverty. It simply means that the family caregivers have failed to meet the children's material needs, so not providing adequate clothing or food or housing or education or medical care or supervision. Those are all grounds for child neglect. Most of the children who are taken come from impoverished or low-income families, and Black children and Indigenous children are disproportionately taken from their families. So, about fifteen percent of Native children will be taken by the time they reach age eighteen. About twelve percent of Black children will be taken by the time they reach age eighteen. An astounding number of families are investigated by Child Protective Services, Black children in particular. A recent study found that more than half of Black children will be subject to a child welfare investigation by the time they reach age eighteen. There are deep roots in this system targeting the most marginalized communities. Again Black and Native or Indigenous communities have been the main targets. For a long time, Black children were simply ignored by the child welfare system, but when Black families began to enter the welfare and child welfare systems, we see that both systems became more punitive. This is where we get the mushrooming of the foster care population with federal policy and state policy turning to family separation as the main way that it addressed the unmet needs of Black children. Of course, totally inadequately because we have a huge child poverty rate in the United States, and we know that the needs of impoverished children aren't met by this system.

But what this system does is pretend it's meeting those needs by putting children in foster care and regulating and policing families, when in fact this is a way of obscuring the need for radical social change and reimagining what we think of as child safety. Let me just add that there are really deep entanglements between the family policing system and the criminal legal system, both practically in the way that they set up joint task forces and in terms of their carceral logic. Caseworkers often bring along police officers to search homes and investigate families and take children away and the carceral logic of punishing people to address human needs and social problems governs the prison system, the criminal legal system, and the family policing system.

Finally, I'll wait for your next question to see if you want to talk about how we abolish these systems because I want to talk about that as well. Let me also mention that the foster care system—the so-called foster care system, which is really a foster industrial complex—is a multi-billion dollar system that maintains children away from their families. Those people who maintain the children away from their families get more benefits than the struggling families themselves, and it is a system that has been shown through multiple studies to be extremely harmful to children. Not only the abuse that many suffer within it, but also the outcomes are really dismal for children in foster care. They are less likely to graduate from high school and go to college, more likely to be houseless, have lower incomes, more likely to be incarcerated or put in juvenile detention, suffer from PTSD and a host of other kinds of harms that come from being taken from your family. That separation itself causes trauma, and they are then put into a system that moves children from place to place, puts far too many in institutions instead of in foster homes and is very disruptive to children's lives.

NGANA: Thank you for that. I'm sure that this was a prolific amount of work that you've done boiled down into a few minutes. When you mentioned talking more about abolition, I saw a lot of heads nodding in the crowd, so let's talk about that. So, a part of addressing these systems is pushing against them. How do we contest the foster industrial complex you were talking about, the family policing system? So, are there any sort of movements or actions rooted in abolition that you are seeing happening today that support this reproductive justice movement?

ROBERTS: Yes, I can talk about some recent developments in abolishing the family policing system, as well as ways in which reproductive justice activists are recognizing ties between their movement and the movement to abolish the prison-industrial complex and also an abolitionist approach to ending the injustices that we see with regard to reproduction in particular. So, let me first just say why reproductive justice should be an abolitionist movement. When you're dealing with a system or a set of institutions and policies that are rooted in false and white supremacist, sexist, heterosexist, ableist, capitalist ideologies that are designed to oppress people, that are designed to obscure the need for social change, you cannot fix these systems. The prison-industrial complex and the system of family policing for example, cannot be fixed because they were grounded in and have continued to support a racial capitalist system, to support white supremacy, to support structures of political inequality, hierarchies of social and political and economic injustice. So, they have to be abolished, which means reimagining the society we want and reimagining how people's needs should be met, how violence should be addressed in our society and prevented, how social conflict should be grappled with in ways that are caring, that support human flourishing, and no longer reinforce the unequal structures that still govern our society.

So, at the same time that we're dismantling the unjust systems, we have to be creating, building the ways of relating to each other and meeting our needs that we want. So, that overall is the approach that is required for reproductive justice, it's required for ending the prison-industrial complex and family policing. The family policing system, for example, is rooted in the ideology that children in impoverished families and families that are living under racist conditions are disadvantaged because of pathologies that their parents have and that the way then to address the children's disadvantages and unmet needs is to take them away from their families and put them into state custody. That's the thinking that the family policing system is grounded in, and even when it is reformed, it is still grounded in that idea. I haven't heard of any reforms within the so-called child welfare system that don't have, at the bottom, the threat of taking your children away from you. I've never heard of any reforms that say we're going to treat wealthy white families the same as Black, Indigenous, and impoverished white families. It's still targeted at the most marginalized communities. Abolitionists are building a better way, a more humane and caring, nonpunitive, noncoercive way of actually supporting families and meeting children's needs.

Another thing I want to emphasize about an abolitionist approach is that you begin to realize that abolitionist movements, including the unfinished movement of the abolition of slavery in America, which requires a truly just and democratic society, the movement to abolish family policing, the movement to abolish the prison-industrial complex—those movements are moving toward a common vision of a just and humane and caring society, and that it makes sense then for us to come together to share strategies, to share activism, to share support for each other. One of the most exciting aspects of an abolitionist framework in activism is that you see more clearly not only the connections among the violent and harmful systems but also the connections among our visions for a better society and therefore the opportunity to work together to create that society.

NGANA: Thank you for that pretty robust explanation of abolition and—I think I'm going to skip one of the questions I have as you're talking about how abolition can bring people together, right, how we can work as a community towards something that is healthier and better for all of us. I'm wondering what sort of advice you have for people wanting to join these efforts, wanting to join reproductive justice movements because the topics that we're discussing right now and the idea of having to abolish and rebuild systems that are so deeply rooted and honestly successful in the way that they were designed can be very overwhelming to think about, right? So I always like to think about what can we do ourselves, here and now, where we are to make it feel more achievable for those us and anybody watching to make incremental change to support reproductive justice. So, to kind of repeat the question, what advice do you have for people wanting to support these movements or join them?

ROBERTS: Let me first respond to what you were saying about being overwhelming and I think it does seem very overwhelming. We're trying to change four hundred years of ideology and foundational ways of living and valuing people that are so, so deeply embedded. This morning I was giving a talk about racism in medicine and the persistence of ideas about Black bodily difference and the notion that race is a natural division of human beings that produces different groups of people who have innate biological differences that explain health and other inequities. That idea has been circulating for four to five hundred years. It's not just about changing institutions and systems, it's also about changing foundational ways of thinking, and boy, race is so foundational to all of what we've been talking about, and these ideas are so widely held. And then there's the backlash movement that wants to prohibit even teaching about this. But number one: I think recognizing that these are not innate traits that people have—even racism is not an innate trait, recognizing that these structures were built, and these ideas were invented means that we can invent something else. It means that they can be dismantled. Just knowing the history and the way in which white supremacy and patriarchy and classism etc. have been built on each other from fundamental foundations also gives us the ability to think about how we can unbuild them, how we can dismantle them, how we can build on a different ideology and way of thinking. So just foundationally thinking about it, I think it's important to recognize that injustice is not natural. It's the view of the oppressor that oppression is natural, that the disadvantages that oppressed people encounter and resist, that they're natural—that's the oppressor's view. That's the view of the elite to try to get us to believe that the injustice and the inequality in our society are natural.

So once we recognize it's not natural, then there opens up the possibility, the real possibility that we can change it. And then we can also look at the long history of resistance. For every unjust way of thinking, there's always been resistance against it. From the very beginning of the invention of race there have been people who said no, God did not create the races. Nature did not divide us into races. There's been resistance by people who were enslaved despite everything against them. They have resisted and succeeded in rebellions. Yes, many rebellions were snuffed out, but there were those that succeeded. So, we have a long legacy of resistance and victories from it. So, that's just to let people know that we can change society. We can abolish these institutions and systems but of course, you use the word *incremental*. I use that as well. It's not going to happen overnight. We do have to strategize about the incremental changes, as Ruth Gilmore says, the non-reformist reforms, the abolitionist reforms that we have to engage in as we work toward the common vision we have of a society that's more humane and equal and caring.

And then the question is: What can I do to contribute to the strategizing and the implementation of those incremental steps? Now, you have to do it with other people; you can't just think about it, you know? You can't just—I mean it is good to donate money, but even then you should donate it to people who are doing the work. So, you have to learn about what abolition means. If you're not clear on what it means, then find abolitionist organizations to work with. This has to be a collective effort because you can't figure out what abolition requires in your head by yourself. If we're trying to change, radically change, hundreds of years of injustice and the kinds of ideas and structures that have built, then it's going to take work to know how to do it; it takes work to organize and strategize. There are so many questions that are unanswered, that you can't turn to a book for, that I'll never be able to answer by myself. And even people who have been doing this longer than I have and are smarter than me can't answer it by themselves. We have to strategize and work together, and so the first thing again after learning about abolition and being committed to it is finding an organization of activists who are doing the work that you're interested in and seeing how you can contribute to it.

NGANA: Yeah, I think that that's a great reminder for us, especially those of us who spend so much time in the academy that we do a lot of reading and thinking and producing of knowledge, right, but sometimes it doesn't always translate into the action piece. So, remembering—and I think that this event does that really well—later in the event we're gonna have more information on how can we be a part of these movements. We have activist organizations like SisterSong supporting this event, so figuring out ways that we can marry these two parts of a lot of who we are, the people sitting in this room, as students and staff and faculty, to read and think but also work with people who are on the front lines doing this work as well. This is a really great reminder, but I wanted to be aware of the time. Part of me wants to tempt fate and ask you to put your video back on, but I'm not sure if that's going to be a good idea. But are we gonna do some questions? Okay, so there are a couple people in the audience who have questions, so I will let the microphone go around. Okay, Professor Roberts, did you want to try your video?

ROBERTS: Okay, I'll try, and I'll turn it off if it messes things up. I'll also just add one thing to what you just said, Colette?

NGANA: Yes.

ROBERTS: Just because you have training in some field and you're really smart doesn't mean you are going to know what is best for the people whom you are trying to serve and whose lives you're trying to improve—they know a lot more than you do. I wouldn't dare to write anything or recommend anything without working with people in the communities I want to serve and with people who are doing grassroots work and know better than I do what the issues are, what the problems are, what's oppressing people in their communities and what are the best ways to address them and working together to figure what those recommendations should be.

NGANA: Wonderful, thank you. So, I'm going to hand it over to audience questions. Over here—

AUDIENCE: Good afternoon thank you, for this eye-opening presentation. I think that going along with what you're saying for next steps for any of us that want to work together with the community to make systems much more humane is a need to be able to tolerate the mistakes that we are going to make along the way. So, to tolerate each other, try to move along despite differences sometimes even language can move people to not be open to others. So if you could talk a little bit more about that, that would be good, thanks.

ROBERTS: Yeah, I think that's important as well. So I think we're talking about two related aspects of doing this work. One is the importance of understanding that you could make a mistake and that therefore you want to get as much input and engagement as you can with the people whose lives you're going to impact with your work and—so it's both because you, to make your work effective, want to work with people who are doing activism, but also the people whose lives will be impacted by it. You have to recognize

"I might make a mistake if I don't do that." But that doesn't mean that we should be willing to jump on people who do make mistakes. I think we need the humility to recognize that, although there are long legacies of resistance, we are moving in uncharted territory. Even right now after the Dobbs decision, the political landscape we're working in is different than it was prior to Roe. As I was engaging with Colette, we've now moved into an era where criminalization of pregnancy is more intense than it was prior to Roe.

So—what does abolition mean in 2023? What do those incremental reforms mean? What is an abolitionist reform and what is a reformist reform? I think we have to have some humility that we don't know easy answers and we have to collectively figure out those answers, but in order to do that we all have to be gracious. I'm not saying we should be tolerant of people who are out to commit oppression, and it also doesn't mean we have to be so nice that we don't want to hold people accountable. It's not that. I took your question to be related to people who are working together on a common mission for social change, and we may have disagreements about how to do that. I've encountered a lot of disagreements among people who want to abolish the family policing system and exactly how can we engage, for example, with child welfare departments. Some people say you can't do it at all, they say no social worker should work with anything having to do with a Child Protection Agency or with a child welfare department. Other people say, "Well we can, under certain circumstances" and other people say, "Well, you've got to have someone in there who can make change from the inside" These are all views that come from people who genuinely want to abolish these systems, and if we become unforgiving and lack humility about it, we won't be able to have these collective efforts. So, I think it's one of those complex aspects of any kind of work that is seeking genuinely to make a real impact.

TRECASA: I think we have reached our time for today, unfortunately, so can we have a round of applause for both of our speakers?

[*Applause*]

TRECASA: We're grateful for the time and your information and we invite our guests to please continue on learning with the Walking Narrative Exhibit next door, the Take Action room, and get a T-shirt, a sticker, or a book. Thank you!

NGANA: Thank you everyone!

Talking Foreign Policy Transcript

Launched in 2012, *Talking Foreign Policy* is a one-hour radio program, hosted by CWRU School of Law Co-Dean Michael Scharf, in which experts discuss the salient foreign policy issues of the day. It airs quarterly on WKSU 89.7 FM in Cleveland and is webcast live for worldwide listening at Ideastream. Archived broadcasts can be accessed anytime through the School of Law YouTube page. Starting in September 2021, *Talking Foreign Policy* is also available as a podcast.[1]

February 21, 2023, broadcast. What Went Wrong in Afghanistan?

Participants
Shannon E. French
Gregory P. Noone
John Sopko
Paul Williams

SCHARF: Since the US withdrawal from Afghanistan in August 2021, the situation has gone from bad to worse. Today, twenty million Afghans are starving, and millions are internally displaced.[2] The Taliban is back in power. They are once again providing sanctuary to terrorist groups.[3] They have decreed that Afghan girls shall not have access to education above the sixth grade.[4] And they have prohibited Afghan women from driving, taking public transport, and holding jobs.[5] In a recent report to Congress, John

---

1. This transcript was created, and footnotes added, by Grotian Scholars Anna Buczek and Jack Sartee.
2. "Afghanistan: Nearly 20 million going hungry," *UN News* (May 9, 2022), https://news.un.org/en/story/2022/05/1117812.
3. *See generally* Seth G. Jones, "Countering a Resurgent Terrorist Threat in Afghanistan," *Council on Foreign Relations* (April 14, 2022), https://www.cfr.org/report/countering-resurgent-terrorist-threat-afghanistan.
4. Diaa Hadid, Taliban begins to enforce education ban, leaving Afghan women with tears and anger, *NPR* (December 21, 2022), https://www.npr.org/sections/goatsandsoda/2022/12/21/1144703393/taliban-begins-to-enforce-education-ban-leaving-afghan-women-with-tears-and-ange.
5. "Afghanistan: Taliban orders women to stay home; cover up in public," *UN News* (May

Sopko, the US Special Inspector General for Afghanistan, wrote: "Unless the US government understands and accounts for what went wrong, why it went wrong, and how it went wrong, it will likely repeat the same mistakes in the next conflict."[6] I'm Michael Scharf, Dean of Case Western Reserve University School of Law.[7] In this broadcast of *Talking Foreign Policy*,[8] our expert panelists, including Sopko, will seek to answer those questions… right after the news.

[STATION BREAK]

SCHARF: Welcome to *Talking Foreign Policy*. I'm your host, Michael Scharf, Dean of Case Western Reserve University School of Law. In this broadcast, our expert panelists will be discussing the Afghanistan debacle. In our first segment we will discuss the goals, strategies, and tactics of the longest war in US history. In the second segment, we will examine what went right and what went wrong. And in the final segment, we'll discuss the lessons learned and apply them to other current conflicts in which the US is engaged. Headlining our panel of experts is Cleveland native and Case Western Reserve Law alum John Sopko,[9] who was sworn in as Special Inspector General for Afghanistan Reconstruction on July 2, 2012. He was appointed by President Obama, served under President Trump, and continues to serve under President Biden. For the last ten years, Sopko and his staff have raised concerns about waste, fraud, and abuse of US assistance funds for Afghanistan, as well as the sustainability and viability of the Afghan government and military ahead of the US withdrawal in 2021. John, thank you for joining us today.

SOPKO: Pleasure to be here.

7, 2022), https://news.un.org/en/story/2022/05/1117762.
6. Oren Lieberman, Natasha Bertrand, and Jeremy Herb, "Watchdog report says Trump and Biden administration decisions drove collapse of Afghan security forces," *CNN* (May 18, 2022), https://www.cnn.com/2022/05/18/politics/afghanistan-watchdog-report/index.html.
7. Michael Scharf is a co-dean of Case Western Reserve University School of Law and the Joseph C. Hostetler—BakerHostetler Professor of Law. He has written and published extensively in the area of international law. Michael P. Scharf, Case W. Reserve Univ. Sch. of Law, https://case.edu/law/our-school/faculty-directory/michael-p-scharf [https://perma.cc/DX5Q-MRPH].
8. *Talking Foreign Policy*, Case W. Reserve Univ. Sch. of Law, https://case.edu/law/centers-institutes/cox-international-law-center/talking-foreign-policy.
9. John Sopko is the Special Inspector General for Afghanistan Reconstruction, appointed by President Obama on July 2, 2012. His experience includes more than thirty years in oversight and investigations, and more than twenty years on Capitol Hill. *John F. Sopko*, SIGAR, https://www.sigar.mil/about/leadership/leadership.aspx?SSR=1&SubSSR=2&Sub2SSR=1&WP=IG%20SIGAR.

SCHARF: And we are also joined by Dr. Shannon French,[10] the Director of the Inamori International Center for Ethics and Excellence at Case Western Reserve University. She was previously a professor at the US Naval Academy and was recently named the General Hugh Shelton Distinguished Chair in Ethics by the US Army Command and General Staff College Foundation. She is the author of the acclaimed book, *The Code of the Warrior: Exploring Warrior Values, Past and Present*. It is great to have you back on *Talking Foreign Policy*, Shannon.

FRENCH: Great to be back, Michael.

SCHARF: And we are also happy to welcome back Dr. Paul Williams,[11] the president of the Public International Law & Policy Group, a Nobel Peace Prize-nominated NGO.[12] Paul has served as legal adviser in twenty peace negotiations and is the author of the recently published book, *Lawyering Peace*. Welcome back to *Talking Foreign Policy*, and this time Paul is actually in our studio in Cleveland.

WILLIAMS: Thank you, Michael. It's a pleasure to be back.

SCHARF: And finally, we are joined from West Virginia by Dr. Greg Noone.[13] He's the director of Fairmont State University's National Security and Intelligence Program. Greg is a retired captain in the US Navy and has served as head of the International Law Branch in the Pentagon. Welcome to our show, Greg.

NOONE: Thank you for having me, Michael.

---

10. Shannon French is Case Western Reserve University's director of the Inamori Center for Ethics and Excellence. She is also a Professor in CWRU's Philosophy department. *Shannon French*, Case W. Reserve Univ. Sch. of Law, https://philosophy.case.edu/faculty/shannon-french/.
11. Paul Williams is a professor at American University Washington College of Law. He is also the president of PILPG, a Nobel Peace Prize nominated NGO that has provided legal counsel in a dozen peace negotiations over the past twenty-two years. *Paul Williams*, Am. Univ. Wash. College of Law, https://www.wcl.american.edu/community/faculty/profile/pwilliams/bio [https://perma.cc/ME9B-SEK9].
12. The Public International Law and Policy Group is a global pro bono law firm that provides free legal services for peace negotiations and post-conflict, war-crimes prosecution, and transitional justice issues. *Public International Law & Policy Group*, https://www.publicinternationallawandpolicygroup.org.
13. Greg Noone is the director of the Fairmont State University National Security and Intelligence Program and an assistant professor of political science and law. Previously, he received a Special Act Award for his work in Afghanistan with the United States Institute of Pease (USIP). *Dr. Gregory Noone*, Fairmont State Univ., https://www.fairmontstate.edu/collegeofliberalarts/dr-gregory-noone.

SCHARF: Let's start things off with Inspector General Sopko. This month, you filed a report to Congress about the current state of affairs in Afghanistan.[14] Can you provide a summary of some of the highlights from your report?

SOPKO: Certainly, Mike. And to say things aren't great in Afghanistan would be an understatement. The situation was grim before the Taliban returned to power and has only gotten worse. So Afghans now face the highest levels of hunger in the world, and two-thirds are dependent on food aid.[15] So, life is worse for Afghans right now, and particularly, in the midst of this humanitarian crisis, the Taliban have increased oppression of women and girls.[16]

SCHARF: So, let's provide some context to this, and I will ask retired Captain Greg Noone to take us back twenty years. Greg, why did the US invade Afghanistan in 2001? Who were we fighting? And who were our allies?

NOONE: Well, and of course all of our listeners know that it was a result of 9/11, but even before 9/11, one of our key allies in the region, the Northern Alliance—their leader, Massoud, was assassinated two days prior to 9/11.[17] We were struck on two days later, and as a result of our ability to project self-defense through the UN charter[18] and our NATO agreement,[19] we then went to Afghanistan shortly thereafter and proceeded to "prosecute the war," as we say in the military. Now, one of the things that we demanded right away from the Taliban was to turn over Osama bin Laden and the al Qaeda members, destroy terrorist camps, and return any hostages they may have had. The Taliban started this kind of negotiation where they wanted proof that Osama bin Laden actually was behind 9/11, and then they offered to turn him over to a third party for trial. So, as a result, that

---

14. Special Inspector General for Afghanistan Reconstruction, "What We Need to Learn: Lessons from Twenty Years of Afghanistan Reconstruction" (2021), https://www.sigar.mil/pdf/lessonslearned/SIGAR-21-46-LL.pdf.
15. *World Bank Survey: Living Conditions Remain Dire for the Afghan People*, World Bank, https://www.worldbank.org/en/news/press-release/2022/11/22/world-bank-survey-living-conditions-remain-dire-for-the-afghan-people.
16. "Afghanistan: Taliban orders women to stay home; cover up in public," UN News (May 7, 2022).
17. *See generally* Catherine Putz, "Ahmad Shah Massoud: An Afghan Napoleon," *The Diplomat,* (Sept. 29, 2021) https://thediplomat.com/2021/09/ahmad-shah-massoud-an-afghan-napoleon/.
18. U.N. Charter art. 51.
19. North Atlantic Treaty art. 5, Apr. 4, 1949, 63 Stat. 2241, 34 U.N.T.S. 243.

ended up being a full-scale invasion with the US leading, and its NATO allies in support, along with the Northern Alliance.[20]

SCHARF: And then let me bring Paul Williams into this. Paul, what was the endgame, the strategic goals? In other words: what was our twenty-year engagement in Afghanistan all about?

WILLIAMS: I think we're still trying to figure that out, Michael. We went in, as Greg noted, in order to hunt down Osama bin Laden, to destroy al Qaeda. For the first two years that was our goal, and then for the next eighteen, we drifted. I'll tell you a quick little story: I was down at the Air War College[21] for a round table "Have a Think" about our Afghanistan policy in the early years of the Obama administration. There was a marine officer who very clearly explained his tactic of how he was going to go to the Helmand province.[22] He was going to clear, and he was going to hold. And then I looked at the foreign policy official, and I said, "Great. And why is he clearing and holding?" No kidding, the answer was "President Obama's very smart. I'm sure he has a plan."

SCHARF: And Paul, just to follow up, what does clear and hold mean actually?

WILLIAMS: Well, essentially it was—and Greg can correct me if I'm wrong on this—a military tactic for the armed forces to go into an area, clear it of hostile forces, clear it of Taliban, hold it (at great risk) for something to then happen—for reconstruction, for democracy-building, for rule of law.[23] But what was shocking was that it wasn't clear why they were clearing and holding, what was our overall strategic objective. And it drifted for eighteen more years.

SCHARF: So then after these eighteen years, why did the US abruptly pull out of Afghanistan?

WILLIAMS: Because we lost.

SCHARF: And, abruptly, that's the way to go with these things?

---

20. *See generally* "The U.S. War in Afghanistan," Council on Foreign Relations, https://www.cfr.org/timeline/us-war-afghanistan.
21. "About Air War College," Air Univ., https://www.airuniversity.af.edu/AWC/.
22. "Factbox: Five facts about Afghanistan's Helmand province," *Reuters* (July 2, 2009), https://www.reuters.com/article/us-afghanistan-helmand-sb/factbox-five-facts-about-afghanistans-helmand-province-idUSTRE5611CW20090702.
23. Michael O'Hanlon, "America's History of Counterinsurgency," Brookings Counter Insurgency and Pakistan Paper Series (No. 4), https://www.brookings.edu/wp-content/uploads/2016/06/06_counterinsurgency_ohanlon.pdf.

WILLIAMS: Well, we can have a conversation about whether that's the way to go or not. But, we would have continued to drag on and on and on. We could've done it better, and we can talk about how we could've negotiated our surrender, how we could've negotiated our loss. Instead, we pretended that it was some sort of victory. We pretended we were holding over to the Afghans, and in fact we weren't prepared to do it the proper way.

SCHARF: Ok, so, a moment ago, John Sopko, the Inspector General, told us about the current state of affairs in Afghanistan. To summarize from his recent report: the Taliban are back in power. Nearly twenty million people in Afghanistan—almost half the population—are facing acute hunger. There are 3.5 million internally displaced Afghans, while 2.7 million Afghans are refugees outside the country. And meanwhile, the Taliban has ordered that all women must cover their faces in public and should only leave their homes in cases of necessity. They have even decreed that girls shall not have access to education above the sixth grade. Women are prohibited to drive, take public transport, or to hold jobs.[24] So, I'm going to turn to Shannon. Shannon, you're a military ethicist, you've worked at the Naval Academy. What must it be like for US and coalition troops who fought in Afghanistan to see the current state of the country, post-withdrawal?

FRENCH: Well, Michael, the word is, "traumatic." That's what it's like. It is very traumatic for those who fought there and for those who were involved in diplomatic roles and various NGO's and others as well.[25] And this has many layers to it. What we're seeing is a lot of what we call "moral injury,"[26] and *moral injury*, in broadest terms, comes from the sense of having betrayed your own values, often against your will in following authority. It also can come concurrently with feeling that leadership has betrayed you, if you think of how we look at the way that we withdrew and the people who are left behind. Also, those who were lost over the twenty years, and those who are left questioning, "What did they die for?," and was anything achieved. All of that leads to an absolute tsunami of moral injury and psychological trauma.

---

24. Special Inspector General for Afghanistan Reconstruction.
25. *See generally* William A. Galston, "Anger, betrayal, and humiliation: how veterans feel about the withdrawal from Afghanistan," *Brookings* (Nov. 12, 2021), https://www.brookings.edu/blog/fixgov/2021/11/12/anger-betrayal-and-humiliation-how-veterans-feel-about-the-withdrawal-from-afghanistan/.
26. Sonya B. Norman and Shira Maguen, *Moral Injury*, US Dept. of Veterans Affairs, https://www.ptsd.va.gov/professional/treat/cooccurring/moral_injury.asp.

SCHARF: Wow. And Colin Powell used to talk about the "Pottery Barn Rule."[27] I think he said, "You break it, you own it." So, Shannon, as an ethicist, would you say the United States is morally responsible for the dismal state of affairs in Afghanistan?

FRENCH: Yes, we are, but of course there's more to it than that. And the reason there's more to it than that, as my colleagues already noted, is it isn't as though Afghanistan wasn't unbroken before 2001. When the Taliban took power in 1996, this was already an awful situation. You mentioned the plight of women and girls in particular. Under the Taliban, that has been a nightmare. Arguably, one of the painful aspects of this entire experience is that we brought hope. We brought the suggestion of a different future. We brought twenty years of saying, "We're going to help you!" and in some cases actually succeeding in helping children and women and girls get different kinds of education and different kinds of experiences. We rebuilt some things and so forth. And then we left. And so, in some ways, hope is the cruelest gift of all.

SCHARF: Well Greg, besides our moral responsibility, from a national security perspective, why should we, as Americans, care about the situation Afghanistan today?

NOONE: Michael, that's a great question, and allow me a moment to follow up on Shannon's point. I was in Afghanistan in early 2003 as the US started talking about invading Iraq, and the Afghans I was working with all said to me, "Please, don't invade Iraq, you'll forget about us." And the only thing I could do was look them in the eye and tell them, "You're absolutely right." Because the resources are going to go to Iraq, and they're not going to stay here. And remember at that time, we were promising a Marshall Plan[28] for Afghanistan. So that idea of hope, from the national perspective, from a national security perspective, the United States values order in the international sphere, as opposed to Putin's Russia that values chaos[29] and the communist Chinese government that pretends to follow

---

27. *See generally* Robert Siegel, "Powell's Cautions on Iraq," *NPR* (Apr. 20, 2004) https://www.npr.org/templates/story/story.php?storyId=1844476.
28. "Marshall Plan, 1948," US Dept of State Office of the Historian, https://history.state.gov/milestones/1945-1952/marshall-plan.
29. *See generally* Arkady Ostrovsky, "Russia risks becoming ungovernable and descending into chaos," *The Economist* (Nov. 18, 2022), https://www.economist.com/the-world-ahead/2022/11/18/russia-risks-becoming-ungovernable-and-descending-into-chaos.

rules but cheats on the rules.[30] So, order is in our national interest. That's why Americans should support international law and what happens out there around the world. And so having a country that's unstable, that has internal strife, that could be a place that could harbor terrorists, a place that could cause a flow of refugees. Those are destabilizing events. And eventually that will push into an area that causes problems for the US national security interest.

SCHARF: All right, so Greg has made the case on why we should continue to care about Afghanistan, maybe why we should continue to be involved in Afghanistan. Paul, do you agree with that?

WILLIAMS: Well I think we need to learn the lessons of what happened in Afghanistan, because we can care about it, we can feel the sense of moral responsibility, but, quite frankly, Michael, there's very little we can do about it. We gave the Afghans two million dollars, twenty years of an American security umbrella, and there was no measurable change in the outcome of the democratic, anti-corrupt, rule-of-law based society.[31] So, yeah sure, we can care about it, but we have no ability to impact it anymore. We should, however, learn the lessons when we think about what comes next in Syria, what comes next in Sudan, what comes next in Ukraine, because we cannot make the same fatal mistakes in those territories and countries that we made in Afghanistan.

SCHARF: Well, that's a great time for us to take a short break. When we return, we'll talk about what went right and what went wrong in Afghanistan.... So stay with us.

[STATION BREAK]

SCHARF: Welcome back to *Talking Foreign Policy*, brought to you by Case Western Reserve University and Ideastream Public Media. I'm Michael Scharf, Dean of Case Western Reserve University School of Law. I'm joined today by the US Special Inspector General for Afghanistan—John Sopko; the president of the Public International Law and Policy Group—that's Paul Williams; the director of the Inamori International Center for Ethics—that's

---

30. *See generally* "China is becoming more assertive in international legal disputes, *The Economist* (Sept. 18, 2021), https://www.economist.com/china/2021/09/18/china-is-becoming-more-assertive-in-international-legal-disputes.
31. *See generally* Carter Malkasian, "What America Didn't Understand About Its Longest War," *Politico* (July 6, 2021) https://www.politico.com/news/magazine/2021/07/06/afghanistan-war-malkasian-book-excerpt-497843.

Shannon French; and the former head of the Pentagon's International Law Branch—retired Navy Captain Greg Noone. We're talking today about the Afghanistan mess. There's not other way to say it. And in this segment of our show, I'd like to focus the discussion on what went right and what went wrong for the United States in Afghanistan. So, let me begin with Inspector General Sopko. You have submitted at least a dozen "Lessons Learned Reports" to Congress. Can you provide us a summary of the top three lessons from your most recent reports?

SOPKO: I'll try to, Mike. It's ironic, a week before the Afghan government collapsed, we issued a report entitled "What We Need to Learn: Lessons from Twenty Years of Afghan Reconstruction" because that was close to the twentieth anniversary.[32] And what we highlighted—major problems or lessons you could say—were that we had an inability on the US government's side to develop a coherent twenty-year strategy. We also had an inability to understand, and to be honest about, how long that mission would take. I think we said we were turning the corner so many times, we turned around like a top. The third issue was that we failed to insure that the things we were spending tens of billions of dollars on, like the Afghan military, would be sustainable when we departed, which they were not. And lastly, we could not and did not account for the impact of the ongoing violence and its impact. And I shouldn't say the last, but really the biggest issue, I think, was the fact that we totally ignored the corruption in Afghanistan and how that impacted our ability to convince the average Afghan that were actually doing something good for them. And that's helped the Taliban to recruit when they saw all of the corruption.

SCHARF: I think it's really helpful the way you packaged that in a way that was so economical and easy to understand. And it's tempting to just dismiss Afghanistan as a total policy failure. But it's not that simple, I think. So John, can you tell us about some of the successes in the US involvement in Afghanistan?

SOPKO: I mean, there were a number of successes, and I'm glad you're highlighting that. But, I think, at some point you should expect some successes because we were throwing so much money at the problem. Remember, we spent more money in Afghanistan on reconstruction than we did on the entire Marshall Plan to rebuild Europe.

SCHARF: And how much would that have been?

---

32. Special Inspector General for Afghanistan Reconstruction.

SOPKO: 146 billion, I think the Marshall Plan was way less than that in Europe. So, obviously some of that stuck—it's like throwing spaghetti on a wall; some of it stuck. Our help for women and girls was an improvement. That was a success. The civil society development was a success. The development of a free and independent press was a success. We increased the literacy rates.[33] We decreased the child mortality rates. We increased the per capita GDP in Afghanistan. But the problem is, basically, all of those successes have disappeared.

SCHARF: So Paul, Afghanistan has been called a bipartisan debacle. What do you consider were the major mistakes of each the administrations, from Bush to Biden?

WILLIAMS: Well, Michael, I think that there were two consistent mistakes all the way through. President Bush had it right, initially—antiterrorism, hunting down al Qaeda, Osama bin Laden. Then he drifted into believing his own propaganda. We were democratizing Afghanistan, we were making strides, we were having success with the rule of law. We weren't. It was propaganda. And that got picked up by Obama and then Trump, and then Biden, I think, saw it for what it was and pulled the plug. The other failure is that I think we wanted more than the Afghan people. We did what we always do. We found the 5% or the 10% of the population that was like-minded with us and our allies, and we created an echo chamber, and amplified it. And we weren't in touch with the other 90% of the population, which apparently weren't that committed to these democratic and rule-of-law successes, or, at least, our version of how one might have rule of law.[34] So, I'm not surprised that it collapsed. We threw a lot of spaghetti at the wall; I don't think any of it stuck.

SCHARF: And I guess some of the things that we did were really making the matter worse. And I have in mind during the Bush Administration, when we instituted the practice of waterboarding Afghan detainees in order to try and find information to prevent the next 9/11.[35] So, let me ask Greg, our military expert, and Shannon, our ethicist. How did that

---

33. "Literacy rate in Afghanistan increased to 43 per cent," *UNESCO* (March 15, 2020) https://uil.unesco.org/interview-literacy-rate-afghanistan-increased-43-cent.
34. Shadi Hamid, "Americans never understood Afghanistan like the Taliban did," *Brookings* (Aug. 23, 2021), https://www.brookings.edu/opinions/americans-never-understood-afghanistan-like-the-taliban-did/.
35. Eric Weiner, "Waterboarding: A Tortured History," *NPR* (Nov. 3, 2007) https://www.npr.org/2007/11/03/15886834/waterboarding-a-tortured-history.

policy of waterboarding affect our mission in Afghanistan? Greg, do you want to start?

NOONE: Yeah, sure. I look forward to Shannon's answer on this as well, but I think she'll agree with me. Not only is torture immoral, illegal, unethical…it doesn't work. So from a pragmatic standpoint, you're applying pressure to people to try to derive certain information, and you're not going to get that information. What you're going to get back is information that people think you want to hear so you'll stop putting them in a painful situation. And really, what it ends up doing, aside from the horrors of that, it then pushes the fence-sitters. Paul just gave percentages of where the Afghan population may or may not have been, but the fact of the matter is there always a significant number of fence-sitters, and they're looking at both sides, and they're trying to figure out which way they should go. So, you torture my uncle, and he comes home and tells the family about it. Well, guess which side we're going to pick after that. The side that tortured him? Or the side that's saying we need to get rid of these people and get our country back. So, it doesn't work is the bottom line, and from a pragmatic standpoint. Shannon?

FRENCH: Well, Greg, I agree with you 100%. It is indeed not just illegal but unethical. And the other point, which you made, is that it's a propaganda boon for our enemies. And not only the enemies that we're fighting in whichever conflict in which we do the act, but obviously this spreads around the world, and it damages our moral authority. It damages trust, not only, again, with enemies, but also amongst allies. And just overall erodes our legitimacy.

SCHARF: So Greg, let me turn and ask you about the role of Pakistan in the Afghan conflict? So, ultimately, was Pakistan an ally or a foe?

NOONE: Well, we like to say Pakistan is a "frenemy." They're both a friend and an enemy. Pakistan is supposedly a major non-NATO ally, but the reality of it is that Pakistan created the Taliban.[36] The Pakistani intelligence services are what actually makes the Taliban go. And part of this is the neighborhood they live in. Pakistan wakes up every day thinking they're going to go to war with India,[37] so they want their back door, being

---

36. See generally Manjari Chatterjee Miller, "Pakistan's Support for the Taliban: What to Know," *Council on Foreign Relations* (Aug. 21, 2021), https://www.cfr.org/article/pakistans-support-taliban-what-know.
37. "Conflict Between India and Pakistan," *Council on Foreign Relations* (Updated May 12,

Afghanistan, run by people that they trust, that they're funding, that they're on the same page with. So, the fact of the matter is, they nurtured the Taliban, they've supported them, they've provided them sanctuary. This really impacted our ability to have any type of effective counter insurgency when people could bounce back and forth over the border. And at the end of the day, where was Osama bin Laden living for years? He was living just down the street from Pakistan's version of West Point.[38] So, there's a reason why we couldn't tell Pakistan when we were conducting the mission to go get bin Laden, because we really cannot trust them in this area.

SCHARF: Shannon, as a military expert about ethics and morality, let me ask you about complaints of US Soldiers that they were trained to fight and then ordered to nation-build—something that was outside their expertise. Is that a fair criticism?

FRENCH: I'm a bit on the fence on this one, because, in reality our troops, across the various branches, are really quite flexible—there is a fair amount of agility and ability to learn different skills even on the fly. And we've shown that historically. So, I'm not overly sympathetic to the argument that they can't switch roles back and forth, because they have, and they do. The bigger problem for me, and I've heard this certainly amongst my friends in the military, is that, as was mentioned earlier, the resources and the focus shifted to Iraq. And when that happened, this sense that you're supposed to be doing nation-building, but you're not our priority anymore, and you can't count from one moment to the next on that support coming back at any point—and we know it didn't—that was what caused more frustration.

SCHARF: And then, John, you mentioned how much we spent. You said it was more than the Marshall Plan, and that was the plan that rebuilt Europe after World War II, so we're talking billion and billions of dollars.[39] Your office was created to combat the waste and fraud in the administration of the US-funded programs In Afghanistan. How much waste and fraud did you uncover?

2022), https://www.cfr.org/global-conflict-tracker/conflict/conflict-between-india-and-pakistan.
38. Tara Kibler, "Secrets of the Serial Set: The Killing of Osama bin Laden," *Heinonline Blog* (May 20, 2020) https://home.heinonline.org/blog/2020/05/secrets-of-the-serial-set-the-killing-of-osama-bin-laden/.
39. Peter Coy, "Afghanistan Has Cost the U.S. More Than the Marshall Plan," *Bloomberg* (July 31, 2014), https://www.bloomberg.com/news/articles/2014-07-31/afghanistan-has-cost-the-u-dot-s-dot-more-than-the-marshall-plan.

SOPKO: Well, we uncovered quite a bit, Mike. And we did a rather intensive look at every report we issued, every indictment we issued, in a timeframe of 2008 to I believe it was 2019. And after this analysis, we determined about thirty percent, and at that time and that period that was only $63 billion, but that's what we determined was subject to waste, fraud, or abuse.[40] We can extrapolate from there, but probably about thirty percent of the money we spent on reconstruction was wasted.

SCHARF: And I've read in your reports the theory of the absorption principle. Can you tell us about that?

SOPKO: The *absorption rate* is a term used in development circles, and it talks about how much money you can give to a country to assist it in comparison to the GDP before that money is probably wasted. Depending on the development of the individual country, it goes anywhere from fifteen to thirty percent. We discovered that when we looked at that and talked to development experts that most of the time we were in Afghanistan, the United States alone was giving more than 100% of the GDP of Afghanistan.[41] What that basically means is the money probably was wasted. And again, regarding absorption rate, the best way—as some scholar described it to me—was to picture a sponge in your kitchen sink. You pour water into it, and it holds the water but all of a sudden it hits a certain point where the water just flows out and that flowing out of the water is basically money that could be wasted in Afghanistan.

SCHARF: So just to give some context to that, how does the thirty percent rate of fraud and abuse compare with the US involvement in other conflicts where we spent a lot of aid money like World War II, Korea, Vietnam, or Iraq?

SOPKO: I would like to answer that question, but I don't think anybody has ever studied that. I know we were asked to do it for Congress, and it was very labor intensive. I know congressmen asked the DoD, State, and AIGs to do it, and as far as I know they never even did it for Afghanistan. I don't think anybody has ever done it for World War II, Korea, Iraq, or Vietnam, so we don't have an answer. But I don't think Afghanistan is an outlier, and probably you have similar rates in those other countries also.

SCHARF: And then John, from your perspective as special inspector general, how badly would you say corruption in the Afghan government undermined the US mission in Afghanistan?

---

40. Special Inspector General for Afghanistan Reconstruction.
41. *Id.*

SOPKO: Mike, that's a good question, and I alluded to it before. We have a tendency to view corruption as just a criminal justice or law enforcement issue. It is not. It is a national security issue, and what we had in Afghanistan was that we created so many corrupt players who were more than just corrupt players. They became the government. They became the oligarchs and the warlords who were abusing the system.[42] The average Afghan basically preferred the Taliban to the corrupt judges, police, and whatever. We sent out there, and so we lost the support and the Afghan government, the central government, lost support to the Taliban. The corruption and the human rights abuses that these oligarchs and warlords in Afghanistan committed basically were used by the Taliban as a recruiting tool, and it was very successful. So at the end you didn't have people who wanted to fight for the Afghan government because it was so bad.[43]

SCHARF: Wow. I hear a theme really emerging here. Instead of winning over hearts and minds, we seem to have done everything possible to lose hearts and minds. Paul, let me then switch over to the issue of the peace negotiations. You have been counsel in over twenty peace negotiations. From your perspective, what was wrong with the Doha agreement and the negotiations?[44] That's the agreement that was signed between the Trump administration and the Taliban in February 2020.

WILLIAMS: Well Michael, I think the fundamental flaws of both the negotiations and the agreement were that they were token. We pretended to have negotiations about a future sustainable Afghanistan where the Taliban would play a role, and we reached an agreement that provided for the Taliban to make a number of commitments that they were never going to abide by. We had an agreement for an intra-Afghan dialogue that the Taliban were never going to consent to and we did not actually really care about. We had lost the war, we wanted to get out, but we pretended that there was somehow an equilibrium, if not a success, and that we had built a nation and we were going to make some room for the Taliban to join into

---

42. JoAnne Allen, "U.S. Indirectly Funding Afghan Warlords: House Report," *Reuters* (June 22, 2010), https://www.reuters.com/article/cnews-us-afghanistan-contract-warlords-idCATRE65L0SK20100622.
43. Special Inspector General for Afghanistan Reconstruction.
44. Julian Borger, Emma Graham-Harrison, Akhtar Mohammad Makoii, and Dan Sabbagh, "U.S. and Taliban Sign Deal to Withdraw American Troops from Afghanistan," *The Guardian* (Feb. 29, 2020), https://www.theguardian.com/world/2020/feb/29/us-taliban-sign-peace-agreement-afghanistan-war.

that national project while we eased our way out. The Taliban saw right through this. I'm not sure we saw right through it. I'm not sure that the military fully grasped the dire straits of the failed nation that we attempted to build or of the military circumstances on the ground and certainly the Trump administration and the State Department didn't grasp that and so when it came time to implement it, the security infrastructure collapsed, and we saw what happened with the Taliban filling that immediate vacuum.[45]

SCHARF: And then John, I know that you issued reports before our withdrawal warning about some of the mistakes you could make in pulling out too quickly. What mistakes ultimately were made in the US withdrawal? Was it inevitable that the government would fall and that the Taliban would take over? What could we have done differently? And we only have a minute for you before the next break.

SOPKO: Well, I would quickly say it became almost inevitable. The warning was that the military was basically hollow. The government was not supported by the people, and we go in great depth in some of our reports, but basically once the troops left, they needed close air support.[46] The Afghan government was the only one that could provide that, and we took the contractors with it. And we predicted and the Air Force predicted that within a matter of months, the Afghan Air Force would collapse. And once that happened, it was over.

SCHARF: And it wasn't even a matter of months, was it?

WILLIAMS: Well, our prediction came in January and so in August by the time the contractors left, it was over.

SCHARF: Well, it's time for another short break. When we return, we'll talk about the lessons learned from the Afghanistan experience. We'll be back in a moment.

[STATION BREAK]

SCHARF: This is Michael Scharf, and we're back with *Talking Foreign Policy*. I am joined today by experts in the continuing crisis in Afghanistan. In this

---

45. Lolita Baldor, "Watchdog: U.S. Troop Pullout was Key Factor in Taliban Success" *Associated Press* (May 21, 2022, 11:14 PM), https://apnews.com/article/afghanistan-biden-government-and-politics-donald-trump-7cef514c6cc96848f61a9e8b7fcdf263.
46. Lynne O'Donnel, "Afghan Air Force Could be Grounded After U.S. Pullout," *Foreign Policy* (June 14, 2021, 2:05 PM), https://foreignpolicy.com/2021/06/14/afghan-air-force-us-withdrawal-taliban/.

final segment, we're going to be discussing the lessons learned and their application to US involvement in other conflicts in the future. Paul Williams, let's begin with you. After nearly two decades of fighting and more than two trillion in US taxpayer funds, after the death of more than 6,000 Americans and 100,000 Afghans, what did we gain from our war in Afghanistan?

WILLIAMS: Michael, we gained an understanding that the United States no longer knows how to do nation-building and maybe should no longer attempt to do nation-building. I know that is not actually your question, but it is something I wanted to say, so I'm going to use that question for it. We spend trillions of dollars on nation-building on a system that simply does not work. We need to get out of that business or develop a new paradigm for what we are going to do in Sudan, Syria, Yemen, and Ukraine. We cannot use the Iraq or the Afghanistan model. It does not work.

SCHARF: Well, let me just follow up, and maybe I'll turn to Greg Noone about this. We did kill Osama bin Laden, the leader of al Qaeda. And I think it seems to me that we knocked al Qaeda on its butt. Greg, are we stronger today versus al Qaeda than we were twenty years ago?

NOONE: The greatest legal answer ever is "it depends," right? The fact of the matter is al Qaeda is dispersed, but you have other groups that are taking its place either in the kind of remnants of al Qaeda or new organizations.[47] So there's always going to be organizations out there like that. You mentioned killing bin Laden. I want to go back to something that Shannon and I talked about. We found bin Laden through good old interrogation techniques. We did not find him through the use of torture.[48] The fact of the matter is we kept interviewing people and interrogating people and there was one individual's name that kept coming up. And everybody got really squirrely around and that name came up and that was the courier and the courier was the connection to where bin Laden was in an isolated location without even internet and any phone service. So I do want to tie that in there that despite some of the things that were done over the course of the war, at the end of the day it was good old-fashioned interrogation that we used to be able to catch the guy that we wanted to catch the most.

---

47. Brian Jenkins, "Five Years After the Death of Osama bin Laden, Is the World Safer?," *RAND* (May 2, 2016), https://www.rand.org/blog/2016/05/five-years-after-the-death-of-osama-bin-laden-is-the.html.
48. Zack Beauchamp, "The Senate Report Proves Once and For All that Torture Didn't Lead Us to Osama bin Laden," *Vox*, (Dec. 9, 2014, 3:10 PM), https://www.vox.com/2014/12/9/7361091/cia-torture-bin-laden.

SCHARF: And I guess what you're saying, Greg, is that we are no better off versus al Qaeda than we would have been had we not invaded Afghanistan.

NOONE: I think there are different ways that we could have undertaken this, and I think Iraq is the real mistake, because that took our eye off the ball. If we were honest about this Marshall Plan idea for Afghanistan, I think we could be in a different place. But once you inserted a full-scale invasion for Iraq for a guy who lives in palaces—guys who live in palaces are always easier to catch than guys who live in caves—and the fact of the matter is we should have engaged in more small-scale operations like we did in in the Philippines down in Jolo[49] that were much more effective against terrorist organizations than a full-scale standing army clear and hold operations type event.

SCHARF: All right, so everybody's heard that we've pulled out. However, the international community is continuing to provide humanitarian aid to people in Afghanistan to meet their shelter, sanitation, their nutritional, and medical needs. But I assume we're not giving any more money now that we pulled out. Is that right, Inspector General Sopko?

SOPKO: You're wrong. We are giving money. We have provided close to eight billion since the Taliban took over. Now, some of it, about two billion, is humanitarian. Some is this $3.5 billion that the Afghan government had at the Federal Reserve, which has now been put into a fund to recapitalize the central bank without giving any assistance to the Taliban, which sounds kind of difficult to do since the Taliban control the Central Bank.[50] And then other money to assist the Afghans who fled. But the important thing is—you talked about the international community. You have to remember we provide most of the funding to the international community, which is kind of ironic. So there is a lot of money being spent by the US government to assist the Afghans, not the Afghan government. You have to be careful about that. We are not supposed to be giving any money to the Taliban but we assume some of it is probably sneaking through.

SCHARF: But we have heard today that the Taliban has totally failed to live up to any of its promises on human rights and counterterrorism back in those

---

49. Patrick Johnson, Gillian Oak, and Linda Robinson, U.S. Special Operations Forces in the Philippines: 2001-2014, RAND (2016), https://www.rand.org/pubs/research_reports/RR1236.html.
50. Jeff Stein, "Biden Aides Seek to Unlock Afghan Reserves Without Enriching Taliban," Washington Post (June 28, 2022, 10:27 AM), https://www.washingtonpost.com/us-policy/2022/06/28/taliban-afghanistan-white-house-money/.

Doha Agreements. So in light of that, John, do you think we should just cut off our assistance and completely disengage from Afghanistan altogether?

SOPKO: That's a very good question but unfortunately—and I don't mean to dodge it, Mike—but we, as IGs, don't do policy. We do process because if we promote a policy, we can't then later go in and assess it or audit it or something. So historically, no IG can do policy. We raised that question in our last quarterly report because we are shipping money in there, and we do know that some of it is going to the Taliban, and we do know that the Taliban is utilizing it both domestically and internationally—the humanitarian assistance—to get better approval ratings among their people. I don't know the answer to that, and that is a big question. That is something the president and Congress really need to look at.

SCHARF: So, I have to say, John, you are about the most candid official I have ever had on this show or met publicly. But let me turn to Paul because your NGO has the word *policy*, in it so you are not afraid to talk policy. What would your answer be? Should we cut off the aid?

WILLIAMS: Michael, we have to be very concerned about continuing the failures of our earlier engagement for the last two decades, and we may be doing that by continuing the assistance. Are we funding a Taliban success story? We funded it, in an odd way, by supporting Kabul over the local governors and local agencies and entities and that, as John noted, pushed people towards the Taliban. Now, the Taliban basically walked into Kabul. They are doing these outrageous actions vis-à-vis the women and the girls, and no one really seems to care except for the women and the girls.[51] And if we are going to fund six billion—if that was what it was—for the Taliban, they are going to be successful. That will undermine our effort to promote democracy and values that we care about in the neighborhood and around the globe.

SCHARF: I see Shannon does care, so I am going to ask you this question. Shannon, the world has rallied to support the Ukrainian people in their struggle against Russia's illegal invasion and occupation. Supporting the Afghan people's current struggle against the Taliban is obviously more complicated. What kinds of support, Shannon, do you think could make a difference?

---

51. "Afghanistan: Taliban Deprive Women of Livelihoods, Identity," *Human Rights Watch* (Jan. 18, 2022, 12:01 AM), https://www.hrw.org/news/2022/01/18/afghanistan-taliban-deprive-women-livelihoods-identity.

FRENCH: The key word that Paul used a minute ago is *local*. One of the many ways to describe the mistakes that we have made is by focusing on anything central because anything central is tied up with the Taliban. It is tied up with corruption. The only kind of help that is going to do any good, and the only kind of engagement that is going to be ethical at this stage is at the very local level where we are helping groups that are still trying to build on the small gains that remain.

SCHARF: All right, so Greg, let me turn to you. Are the women in Afghanistan protesting the draconian restrictions of their rights that have been imposed by the Taliban government? I haven't seen anything on the news, but it could be that the Taliban is just blocking us from seeing it. What is your take on that?

NOONE: Protests are becoming rarer and rarer since the Taliban returned to power, highlighted by violence, highlighted by torture and abuse.[52] When people are in custody, and particularly for women, a social stigma comes with doing something like that. I will say this, going back to the last two answers, I think if the American people knew that eight billion dollars was going to the Taliban, they would lose their minds.

SCHARF: Well, Greg, they are hearing it now on *Talking Foreign Policy*, so the cat's out of the bag.

NOONE: Yeah, and I hope the wider listening audience hears that because the fact of the matter is that Shannon's points are excellent ones about working locally but that's not how the Taliban works. I mean the Taliban is going to have their fingers in every pot. Unfortunately, in an environment like that, there's a lot of grease payments that go around extending the culture of corruption, which has such a pernicious and negative effect on any development. And we would be just pouring in good money after bad money after good or however the phrase goes. And to Paul's point, we are just continuing this failure.

SCHARF: What I suppose what you are saying also is that the situation in Afghanistan is qualitatively different than the situation, for example, in Iran. We are seeing in Iran and Saudi Arabia and in other countries throughout the Middle East this wave of women rising up and standing up against this

---

52. Washida Amiri, "Women, Protest and Power—Confronting the Taliban," *Amnesty International* (Mar. 7, 2023), https://www.amnesty.org/en/latest/campaigns/2023/03/women-protest-and-power-confronting-the-taliban/.

anti-woman type of draconian measures that these countries have. So let me turn to Shannon. Do you think that we are seeing something larger here that might actually bleed over to Afghanistan? Are we on the cusp of a global rejection of extreme interpretations of Islam that deny women autonomy? Could this be sort of like the Arab Spring?

FRENCH: Well, I brought up hope in a negative way previously. Here, I am going to have a bit of hope. I would love to see that be the case, obviously, and I do think that to the degree that the word gets out from country to country, it certainly does strengthen these movements to know that they are not alone and that this is happening in countries around the world. One of the biggest challenges, though, and this is something that we have to confront, is that those of us in the West who would love to be very supportive of the idea of this kind of change for women's rights cannot do so in a way that makes it look as though the West is the driving force. That only undermines these women who are working so hard in their countries for this kind of change and puts them at greater risk and greater danger. We cannot in any way be seen to be instigating any of it or pushing it from behind. All we can do is try to lift their voices.

SCHARF: I think the most distressing thing about this conversation is that I am left with the view that there really is not much we can do to help right the situation in Afghanistan and that it continues to get worse and worse. So, I suppose the lessons learned are best used for other situations around the world. And in the last few minutes, what I would like to do is have each of the panelists tell us what you think the lessons are from Afghanistan for US involvement and other current conflicts such as Ukraine, Syria, Yemen, and Myanmar. And I am going to start out with Inspector General Sopko. Do you think that we should be creating a special Inspector General for Ukraine?

SOPKO: I personally think we should, because we have had a success, I think, with Iraq, with the SIGIR, the Special IG for Iraq Reconstruction, and I think without tooting my own horn, with Afghanistan.[53] It is set up to focus on a lot of money being spent in a country in a war zone and you need to have support and oversight there immediately. And, being a special IG, you go out of business at some point, but you are mainly focused on

---

53. Stuart Bowen et al., "Learning From Iraq: A Final Report From the Special Inspector General for Iraq Reconstruction," Defense Tactical Information Center (Mar 2013), https://apps.dtic.mil/sti/pdfs/ADA587236.pdf.

that one country. And I think that is helpful, and I know there's a lot of similarities between Ukraine and Afghanistan. There's a lot of dissimilarities. and I do not want to say Afghanistan and Ukraine are the same, but we are pouring a tremendous amount of money very quickly into Ukraine. I think we have poured in about $113 billion to Ukraine in one year, and at that pace I think after eighteen months we will spend more money in Ukraine than we did in all of Afghanistan for twenty years.[54] So you've gotta focus on it and the problem of spending too much too quickly with too little oversight is something that should be sending red or orange lights blinking somewhere in the Pentagon and in Congress.

SCHARF: I am actually really surprised to hear that we do not have an Inspector General for Ukraine given how much money that we are spending there. Let me turn it to Greg Noone. What is the lesson learned in your mind?

NOONE: I think the lesson is that we cannot abandon our allies in the field. And if you do, the next time you need allies, you may not have any. And what I am specifically talking about with respect to Afghanistan is the debt that we owe to the interpreters and the fixers and people that stepped up and joined us when we asked people to step up and join us.[55] It does not mean blindly, mindlessly continuing failed policy but you have to make sure that you are taking care of the people that that have stepped in and agreed to be on your side.

SCHARF: Shannon French, what is your lesson learned?

FRENCH: Well, this won't shock you coming from an ethicist, Michael, but we need to be consistent in making our actions match our values, and that means don't keep making deals with devils. We don't want to continuously undermine our own policies and our own goals by compromises that compromise us and what we are supposed to stand for. So that would be a core point. I would also just want to echo something that my colleagues have all said in one way or another and that this point about focus. I too keep coming back to 2003 and the invasion of Iraq and wonder what the storyline would have been with Afghanistan if the invasion in 2003 had

---

54. Louis Jacobson, "One Year into Russia's War in Ukraine: A Look at U.S. Aid, and Why the U.S. is Involved," *Politifact* (Feb. 23, 2023), https://www.politifact.com/article/2023/feb/23/one-year-into-russias-war-in-ukraine-a-look-at-us/.
55. Jessica Donati, "Majority of Interpreters, Other U.S. Visa Applicants Were Left Behind in Afghanistan," *Washington Post* (Sept. 1, 2021, 4:07 PM), https://www.wsj.com/articles/majority-of-interpreters-other-u-s-visa-applicants-were-left-behind-in-afghanistan-official-says-11630513321.

not happened. And as I look at that, I think again with Ukraine, with all these other conflicts that we have referenced, if we take our eye off the ball, if we allow our focus to shift as too often we do, then I think we are going to reap some more bad news.

SCHARF: And Paul Williams, I am going to give you the last word.

WILLIAMS: Well, Michael, we have to return to American foreign policy driven by our own strategic interests. What we learned from Afghanistan is that we asked men and women to risk their lives. Thousands died, tens of thousands were injured for things that were not necessarily in our strategic interest.[56] We had lost the focus. Sure, rule of law, economic growth, education are all very important in Afghanistan. Why was that an American strategic interest? So when we look at Yemen, Libya, Sudan, Syria, and Ukraine, and we start to develop these additional Marshall Plans or deploying American troops, we need to do it only for things that are in America's strategic interest. I am not sure we know what is in our strategic interest in these countries. We have more clarity in Ukraine which, I think, is one reason why there is such an investment of time, energy, weapons, and resources.[57] But until we can have a clear-eyed assessment of why we are putting these human and financial resources on the ground and risking the lives of our soldiers like we did in Afghanistan, we are going to continue to fail and not succeed where we must if we want to be able to provide a world that we dream of and hope for.

SCHARF: All right, well, it is time to bring our program to a close, and I would like to thank our experts for being with us today and helping us make sense of the crisis in Afghanistan and the implications for the future. It is pretty bleak, I have to tell you. And I think things are just going to get worse and it is going to tug at our heartstrings, but this panel of experts does not think that there is all that much more the United States can be doing. And in fact maybe there is less. We should not be pouring in financial aid continuously to a situation where the Taliban controls the purse strings. So Mr. John Sopko, Dr. Shannon French, Dr. Paul Williams, and Dr. Greg Noone, thank you all for providing your insights about this important topic. I am Michael Scharf, and you have been listening to *Talking Foreign Policy*.

---

56. Ellen Knickmeyer, "Costs of the Afghanistan War, in Lives and Dollars," *Associated Press* (Aug. 17, 2021, 4:12 AM), https://apnews.com/article/middle-east-business-afghanistan-43d8f53b35e80ec18c130cd683e1a38f.
57. Jonathan Masters and Will Merrow, "How Much Aid Has the U.S. Sent to Ukraine? Here are Six Charts," *Council on Foreign Relations* (Feb. 22, 2023), https://www.cfr.org/article/how-much-aid-has-us-sent-ukraine-here-are-six-charts.

Contributors

Madeline Chung is a health disparities researcher from Case Western Reserve University. She serves as a patient caregiver and is the Editor-in-Chief of The Dose Newsletter at UAEM, an international student-led organization that aims to improve global accessibility and affordability of life-saving medicines and research products.

Nikki Coleman is a space ethicist with the Australian Space Agency and a veteran of the Royal Australian Air Force, where she was the Senior Chaplain Ethicist.

Fabio Silva is professor of software engineering at the Federal University of Pernambuco in Recife, Brazil. He is the coordinator of the Artificial Intelligence Excellence Centre for Health and Well-being (SABIÁ) headquartered in Recife.

Corrylee Drozda is an immigration attorney who advocates for low-income immigrants, families, and asylum seekers. She currently serves as a staff attorney at The Legal Aid Society of Cleveland.

Shannon E. French is the Inamori Professor in Ethics, Director of the Inamori International Center for Ethics and Excellence and professor of philosophy and law at Case Western Reserve University.

Richard Herman is an immigration attorney and activist. He is the founder of Herman Legal Group headquartered in Cleveland, Ohio.

Lucas Maciel is a first-year student at Case Western Reserve University studying math, physics, and philosophy.

Sospeter Muchunguzi is an assistant lecturer at the Eastern Africa Statistical Training Centre in Tanzania. He is a doctoral candidate in Management studies in the department of General Management at the University of Dar es Salaam Business School.

Colette Ngana is a doctoral candidate in the department of sociology at Case Western Reserve University. She also serves at the chair of the board of directors of Preterm in Cleveland, Ohio.

Girma Parris is a visiting assistant professor in the department of political science at Case Western Reserve University. His research focuses on the relationship between race and immigration on education and integration.

Dorothy E. Roberts is the George A. Weiss University professor of law and sociology and the Raymond Pace and Sadie Tanner Mossell Alexander professor of civil rights. She also serves as the professor of Africana studies and director of the Penn program on race, science and society at the University of Pennsylvania.

Michael Scharf is co-Dean of the Case Western Reserve University Law School, the Joseph C. Hostetler-BakerHostetler Professor of Law, Director of the Frederick K. Cox International Law Center, and host of *Talking Foreign Policy*.

Mykyta Storozhenko is a PhD student in the department of philosophy at the University of Kentucky.

Caroline Walsh is a PhD student in leadership studies at the University of San Diego. She is a former CIA intelligence officer and a US Coast Guard veteran.